Opie Percival Read

Odd Folks

Opie Percival Read

Odd Folks

ISBN/EAN: 9783743349025

Manufactured in Europe, USA, Canada, Australia, Japa

Cover: Foto ©ninafisch / pixelio.de

Manufactured and distributed by brebook publishing software (www.brebook.com)

Opie Percival Read

Odd Folks

"ODD FOLKS",

BY

OPIE READ,

AUTHOR OF "A CAPTAIN'S ROMANCE."

F. TENNYSON NEELY,   114 Fifth Avenue,
NEW YORK.   PUBLISHER.   MDCCCXCVII.

Copyrighted, 1897,
in the
United States
and
Great Britain,
by
F. TENNYSON NEELY.

(All Rights Reserved.)

CONTENTS.

	PAGE
THE SUPERINTENDENT'S EXAMPLE	5
THE BRICK OFFICE	30
THE GREEK GOD BARBER	41
UGLY RACHEL	52
THE MOON IN THE PICTURE	62
HIS SIXTEEN-EIGHTY-NINE	95
BIG HEP AND LITTLE LADY	108
AN IVORY SMILE	120
OLD JOBLEY	133
OLD BILLY	140
SWINGING IN THE DUSK	146
A MEMORABLE MEAL	153
A DEAD MARCH	156
AN IMPERIOUS COURT	159
HIS SPECIAL	165
AT THE SPRING	177
NOT FOR THREE HUNDRED THOUSAND	183
HER SWEET DREAM	194

ODD FOLKS.

WANTED A CERTIFICATE.

At a small town on a railway running through Kentucky an express company had been robbed of $5,000. The loss of the money was insignificant when viewed simply as the removal of so many pieces of paper bearing the portrait of a distinguished American, but the necessity to hold up some one in the glaring light of the law as a dazzling example was a momentous consideration. It may be observed that a great corporation never knows an evil doer as an individual, but regards him wholly as an "example"; indeed, the closest relationship and services that have endured through many years can be forgotten by a great institution when it sets out to establish an "example." And I have often wondered why some one has not taken up the business of professional "example," to undergo a sentence to prison, for a reasonable salary. Well, $5,000 was taken one night from the express office in Springdale. The safe was blown open, the town trembled for three days in a delirium of excitement, and the agent, with a bruise on his head, lay in his room at the tavern. At that time I was operating a detective agency in Louisville (truly, a despicable calling, I must say), and the division superintendent of the express company sent for me. A great man was he. Consciously impressive, portly, with animal life running like an engine within him. As I entered his private apartment he turned in his chair and, looking at me a moment, said:

"So you are Capt. Blake?"

"My name is Blake; yes, sir."

"I suppose you have heard of our little affair down in the country?"

"Yes; I have read an account of it."

"What do you think?"

"It is only now, sir, that I have found it to my advantage to think."

"Ah; I see." And after a short pause he added: "Now, I tell you what we have done, and then I'll tell you what we want you to do. The agent at Springdale has been arrested."

He paused and looked at me as if he expected me to show astonishment, but I didn't. I simply said: "Yes;" and he continued: "About six years ago he came to us most highly recommended, strictly sober, and with no bad habits. There is no bank in the town, and on numerous occasions he has been intrusted with large sums of money. He is of a good family, and during many years his father has been cashier of a bank in this city."

He leaned back in his chair, stroked his side whiskers, and looked at me, and I fancied that I could hear the great engine of health pumping within him. "I authorized his arrest last night," he went on, "and I have a dispatch telling me that the town is greatly excited. The physician is unable to decide whether or not the blow on the head was self-inflicted, but he agrees that it looks suspicious."

"Well," said I, "what do you want me to do?"

"I have a scheme," he answered. "There have been so many similar cases, you understand, that I believe we could convict him upon the testimony of the physician and other suspicious circumstances; and although it is necessary for us to have an example, you understand, yet I should like to know beyond question whether or not he is guilty. I may be overparticular, but, the fact is, I want him to make a confession. I may be a trifle soft-hearted, you understand, but I'd like to know."

"Don't you always want to know," I asked.

"Oh, yes, surely," he quickly replied, "but as a general thing we are willing for the law to settle that point and act accordingly. But down in that part of the country an example is badly needed, and if this fellow Haines could be brought to confess, why it would be—well, it would be a good thing for us, you know."

"And your scheme?"

"Is this. I want you to be put into the cell with him, win his confidence, and worm a confession out of him."

"Rather an old scheme," I was bold enough to reply.

"Oh, I've been told you are a most discouraging man, but I am determined upon this, and I am willing to pay handsomely for your services, and if you succeed the amount of compensation shall be doubled."

This, of course, interested me, and during more than an hour we laid our plans and talked them over, and when I left him it was with these words: "You may depend upon it that I shall do my duty."

That evening an officer conducted me along the main street of Springdale. The sight of the handcuffs upon my wrists caught the eyes of the corner loungers, and soon a crowd was following us, and occasionally I heard the remark: "Got him all right, haven't they?" I heard the words, "horse thief, I bet you," and as unimpulsive as I am I turned around to confront a mottled face. The officer, who knew nothing of the Superintendent's scheme—who was proud to be made so important—gave me a jerk, and the mob applauded him. By the time we reached the jail the air was full of " horse thief." I had no sooner been shoved through the door into the corridor than the words " hang him " smote my ears like a blow from a mallet, for I knew the abhorrence in which my countrymen held the stealing of a horse; that, charged with any other crime, a man might hope for some sort of a hearing, but that to be suspected of horse theft was more than likely to mean deaf ears and quick action. The mob was now fierce. The jailer, a fat and humorous old fellow, stepped out. I stood in the corridor just behind him. Near me stood a man holding a key waiting to show me to my quarters.

"Boys," said the jailer, "what do you want?"

"You know what we want, Buck," replied a lank fellow who had assumed command outside. "We want that hoss thief!"

"Bill, there ain't no hoss thief here!"

"Tell that up at Bear Waller an' up the right fork of Big Sandy, but don't tell it to us. That feller stole the Widder Cage's hoss, and we want him."

"Who says so?"

"Why, Ab, here." And I saw him nod at a fellow standing near, and the light held at an upper window fell upon his mottled face.

"How do you know, Ab?" the jailer asked.

"Why, McGee 'lowed he was the man, and he was with the fellers that got after him."

"Where's McGee? Let him identify him. And if he's the man, I'll agree to hang him myself, and then eat a foot of the rope. No, boys, you are wrong this time. You have hung fellers out of here all right enough, but you'd make a mistake this time, and it ain't exactly right to make such mistakes. I ricollect they hung the wrong man over at Hover not long ago, and it caused a good deal of talk and some ill-feelin', so I advise you to be more particular. Now, if you want to know right bad, I'll tell you what the man is charged with."

"Out with it," the leader cried.

"Why, they do say that he killed a man."

The light was still held at the window, and I saw the eager and expectant countenance of the leader droop to disappointment.

"Buck, is that straight?'

"As a rope pullin' a bucket out of a well."

"All right, then," said the leader, turning about. "There air occasions when a feller's got a right to kill a man, but nobody ever had a right to steal a hoss. Boys, let's go down to Tobe's grocery. I understand they air goin' to cut a watermillon, knock a nail keg in the head, and wring a dishrag down there pretty soon. Come on."

The jailer, his fat sides shaking, stepped back and closed the door, and the man with the key motioned me to follow him.

As the turnkey was fumbling with the lock I heard the nervous pacing, to and fro, of a man inside the cell, and when I stepped in he turned about, looked at me, and, withdrawing his brief attention with a contemptuous bat of his eyes, said to the jailer:

"Buck, you've been acquainted with me long enough to know that I don't want to be shut in here with a horse thief."

"Oh, you heard them fellers, did you? Of course, you don't want to be shut up with a hoss thief—don't want to be shut up at all for that matter, Jimmie—but there are some things we can't help, and bein' shut up with the first feller that comes along is sometimes one of them. Tom, stick that candle up there over the door and leave it there till it burns out so these here gentlemen can see how to entertain each other. That's all right; it'll stick. Well, good-night. Glad we've got room enough in there for both of you, and if you don't find bed clothes enough shout for more. In fact, whatever you don't see in the dark, ask for."

The shooting of the bolt sent a chill through me, and my fellow-prisoner, noticing my momentary distress, gave me a kindly look. "You are not used to it," he said. "They may be lying about you as they are about me. It's an easy thing to do."

"And sometimes a hard thing to disprove," I replied, sitting down on my bunk, opposite his own. He made no reply, but turned about and resumed his pacing up and down the cell. I was careful not to let him catch me gazing at him, but I sat there studying him closely. And surely I was never impressed more deeply by the bearing and the countenance of a man. There was something about him that was more than graceful, an attraction new to me, unexpected, surprising. I had seen studied suggestions of it on the stage—the handsome, brave, reckless gambler. His features were not regular, his nose was faulty, his chin weak, and yet as a whole his face was strikingly picturesque. He must have been about twenty-five years of age.

The flickering of the light told me that the candle was dying. Had he been walking so long in silence, and had I in silence been studying him so long?

"We'll soon be in the dark," I said. "I hate the dark. But it is in keeping with this miserable hole. Here a sunbeam would be like a bright-haired child, strayed into a den of vice."

"Yes," he replied, pausing to look at me.

"Were you ever on the stage?" I asked.

"No. There goes the light."

Blackness fell about us. I heard him stretch himself

upon his bed. I lay down to ponder over him, to speculate upon his character. I wondered if he were really guilty. Before seeing him I would have staked anything upon my belief in his guilt, but now I was uncertain. Time and again I turned over, striving to force myself to sleep. And I muttered charges of weakness against myself. He had done a rare thing— had won my friendship.

CHAPTER II.

Long before the sun came up, but when the misty dawn-light began, like a thin fog, to stream down from a high and narrow window, my fellow-prisoner arose and resumed his walk. And with a strange impatience I waited to see if daylight would confirm the impression that had come upon me as the dying candle rays were flitting upon the gloomy walls. But before the day was strong there came footsteps down the corridors. The slide-window in the door was opened, and the thick voice of the fat jailer was poured in upon us.

"Boys, stirring about already? Don't believe it's a good plan to stir about much before you eat a bite. Had an uncle that broke a colt before breakfast and aged so fast afterwards that he died at ninety. Bring the wedding breakfast this way, Nick. Our cook got married this morning while the water was boiling. Hah, how's our hoss thief this mornin'? Came in one of bein' a nightmare yistidy evenin', eh? Yes, sir; durin' the off season of the year, when the boys ain't got much to do, they'd as soon hang a man as not. But they don't mean no particular harm by it."

Thus he talked while the turnkey "spread" our breakfast, and he stood there, his great round face filling the window, until breakfast was cleared, and even then he hung about until it grew light enough for me to see him wink. And this he did several times, slyly looking at me and then at Haines. In his "squint" was legible the fact that he had been intrusted with the secret of my mission, and I cannot say that it was an agreeable discovery. I fancied that I could already see unconscious betrayal stewing through his hanging jowl, and, hardened as I was, I must have blushed, for I grew sick at the thought of standing exposed before that young fellow, meeting the contemptuous look of his melancholy eyes. Then the daylight had confirmed the impression left by the dying candle.

The day wore along, and our acquaintance made but slow progress. I waited for his advances, but he made none. When not walking he sat where the light was strongest, reading a lead-colored pamphlet.

"What are you reading?" I asked.

"A fool thing."

"Who wrote it?"

"A fool."

"Ah, I didn't know that a piece of my work had found its way into this place." He laughed. "I suppose it might just as well have been yours, but it happens to be mine—an amateur play printed at my own expense."

"Has it been played?"

"Yes; had a one-night run in the church for the benefit of the same."

"Was it a success?"

"Quite. Respect for the church debt forbade any one's leaving the house, although there was a good deal of tittering when the moon got out of order, burned the negro's fingers, and fell down."

"What's the name of the piece?"

"'The Detective.'"

"I suppose you make him a hero."

"No; a black-hearted villain."

"Served him right," I replied; and it was well that he did not look up, for I felt a slow shiver creeping over me.

At night another candle was placed above the door, and sitting in its yellow glow he grew more inclined to talk seriously of himself. He had been well educated, had tried to do a number of things, had done ill—had failed as a country editor, had learned telegraphy, and at last had settled down to a lonely midnight luncheon in the wayside office of an express company. I was sorry for him, for I knew that hidden somewhere a success might lie waiting for him, as it does for many of us; but, ah, how long it lies waiting, and how rusty it has grown when sometime we find it! His features, now that I had become better acquainted with them, were weaker, and this increased my pity; but I was resolved to do my duty, I would win him if I could.

The days passed and he called me Dick. We had read the same books. In our admiration for the same book or poem lies the first tottering of many a downfall. In a similar taste we recognize our second self, and shrewdness shuts its eyes and dreams.

We talked about books, and those of his favorites that I had not seen I pretended to love. It was night, and the candle was burning above the door.

"A man must live with one self and write with another," he said.

"We all have two selves," I replied. "I know that I have. One self does wrong, and the other self, which is a sort of indulgent parent, suffers over it."

He looked at me and was silent. A shadow fell across his face. He looked up at the candle and said: "We'll soon be in the dark."

"We are always in the dark," I answered. "In darkness while we are doing, and only step out into the light long enough to look back and find that we did a wrong while in the dark. I would give half my life if I could recall one dark night."

He leaned toward me. "What happened?" he asked hoarsely.

"I don't know but I might as well tell you. A trouble aired is lighter for the airing. It is the secret trouble that eats the heart. I am here suspected of a crime."

"Yes?" he said, eagerly.

"But there is no direct proof against me. Come closer. That fat jailer might be out there."

He did not get up; he scrambled across the floor and sat down near me.

"I had been out of employment a long time," I went on, speaking low, "and was forced to quit the city. I wandered about doing odd jobs, desperate, hating the world. Well, one day, not long ago, I came into a neighborhood not far from here. I stopped at a farmer's house and asked for something to eat. He received me into his house, placed a chair at his table, and treated me as his guest. A rainstorm came up, and he insisted upon my remaining over night with him. Just before bed time a hired man came in to receive his wages, and I saw the old man take out his wallet, and when he had unwound a string, laying it carefully across his knee, I caught sight of a $50 note.

Soon afterward I was shown to a room just above. And I laid there thinking of that money. At first I turned over with a shudder. And then the weary miles I had walked stretched out before me. I could see the dust in the road—and the heat danced on the hot hilltop, and in the glimmer I saw that old man's money. I turned over again—not with a shudder, but with a mere shiver—and I saw myself treading that dry road; and I saw a railway train sweeping past, and I caught sight of two men as they tipped their glasses. They saw me, and one of them shouted: 'Not for you, poor fool. I rob the poor, but you haven't sense enough to rob even the rich when they spread their money before your very eyes.' It seemed that the train slacked long enough for the scoundrel thus to tantalize me, and then it thundered on, the two scoundrels tipping their glasses again. I got out of bed, tiptoed to the head of the stairway, and listened. I heard the ticking of the clock. I stepped back and dressed myself. Then I trod softly downstairs. In the room a light was burning dimly. The old man and his wife were sound asleep. His trousers were under his pillow. Slowly I pulled them away, and without noise I got out. Then I ran for a mile at least, and then I stopped and thrust my hand into the pocket—and there was the wallet. The moment I touched it I would have given half my life never to have seen it. But repentance was now too late. I could have taken the money back—in fact, I was almost decided on this risk, when my blood shot through me at the barking of a dog—and dropping the trousers, but gripping the money, I leaped over a fence and ran fiercely into the woods. Well, I went to a town, tricked myself out in new clothes, had my beard shaved off, and was ready to take a railway train and tip glasses with some other scoundrel when I was arrested. I said I was suspected of the crime, and that is the case, for that blessed old farmer was not certain that I was the man. And here I have told you all about it. But I trust you; I don't know why, but I do."

The candlewick fell and the cell was black. Haines said not a word. I heard him scramble to his feet, and then with a sigh he lay down heavily upon his bunk. And so long a silence followed that I thought him asleep, when he began to mutter something and I heard him repeat my own words: "A trouble aired is lighter for the airing."

"I hope you don't think any less of me," I remarked.

"No, I am sorry for you—sorry that your better self yielded. But don't you think they will convict you?"

"Yes, I am afraid so."

"And if they do, are you going to make a confession?"

"No. I have confessed to you, and that was cooling

to my conscience. There is bravado in confessing to the world, but confessing to a friend is a simple virtue."

I listened with my head off the pillow, and he muttered something, but I did not understand him.

"There is one thing I am glad of," said I.

"What is that?"

"The fact that I have no near relatives to be disgraced."

"That's fortunate," he replied.

I waited for him to say more, but he was silent, though I knew that he was not asleep, for I heard him turn over time and again. I was now almost out of patience. I had made my confession. Why didn't he make his? I felt that I had won his confidence; I knew that he admired my tastes, because they agreed with his own. I had given to him the most pronounced of all flattery—I imitated his accent and his mannerisms. I was growing weary of my contract. Confinement was telling on my nerves. Inwardly I cursed the Superintendent and all his senseless whims. I condemned the undertaking as a foolish experiment, without the possibility of a compensating result. But the Superintendent's promise came back to me. My affairs had been running behind hand. I was in need of money. Yes, I would stick it out. Haines began to mutter.

"Talking to me?" I asked.

"No, wasn't saying anything. By the way—and you please pardon me for such a question, but if they should send you to the penitentiary, how long do you suppose it would be for?"

"Not so loud," I cautioned.

"There are no other prisoners on this floor. How long do you suppose it would be for?"

"Ten years at least."

"That long? Terrible to think of. But I suppose robbery is different from theft or embezzlement. After all, if a man goes to the penitentiary it doesn't make much difference for how long. The mere sentence is enough to break his heart."

"Yes, but time may heal a broken heart."

"Not time done in a penitentiary."

Was he laughing at me? I listened, and I thought I heard him titter, but it might have been the ripple of a suppressed sob.

"I wonder what time it is?" said he, turning over wearily.

"Must be nearly day. You seem more than usually distressed."

"I am. My heart has been growing heavier since you told me your story."

"Don't think of me, my dear boy, but of yourself."

"I am thinking of myself, and that's what makes my

heart so heavy." For a few moments he was silent and then he continued:

"And you say there is a sort of bravado in confessing to the world?"

"Yes; and the church, early in the beginning, recognized in man the yearning, the necessity to confess his errors to an individual. In my case religion plays no part. I told you of my depravity and my heart has become lighter. Suppose we go to sleep."

"I can't, Dick, I am too wretched. And now I am going to tell you something—but it's daylight, and our fat friend is coming."

CHAPTER III.

DURING all that day we talked in closest sympathy, but I was afraid to remind him of his resolve to confess. Nor did he refer to it; indeed, at noontime, when sunlight fell into the cell, he flipped a joke at our condition, but I knew that this was broad-day banter and that the ghost would return at night.

That afternoon his sister came from Louisville. On a chair, brought for her by the jailer's wife, she sat inside the cell, and, looking at her, I could have fancied that she was a part of the noon hour. She wept at first, but she grew cheerful when I assured her that her brother would prove his innocence.

"Oh, I know that," she said; "but think of what a shame it is to keep him shut up here so long. And you haven't done anything, either, have you? I don't see what makes people so mean."

She remained with us until evening, and the light was surely gone when she went away; and the hours were slow and long before the candle was put above the door. But the old fellow came with it after a stretched-out season. "Boys," he said, filling the window with his face, "I've a little piece of news for you. The grand jury met to-day and court will be in session before the week's out, and, consequently, you'll have a hearin' pretty soon. But don't git skeered, for the foreman of the jury is a hoss doctor, and the Judge owns a livery stable. This might not seem to make any difference, but it do, for I want to tell you that a feller that knows how to handle a hoss knows how to handle a man.

"Well, I must leave you now," he continued. "Pardon me for not spendin' more time with you, but they keep me on the rush these days."

He was gone at last. Haines was pacing the floor. Would he wait for the death of the candle? I said nothing, but sat on my bunk waiting.

"The candle burns longer than usual to-night," he said. He was waiting for the darkness.

"Yes; for it seems to know that we are sleepy, and it wants to tantalize us."

"I'm not sleepy," he replied quickly. He sat down. I said nothing. "I'm not sleepy—I can't sleep until I have told you something. I'm going to throw off all reserve and talk to you as I would to myself. My father is cashier of a bank. He is one of the most lovable of men, but he is weak, always itching to better his condition in life, living in the midst of money, daily noting its power, counting the wealth of other men. In such an atmosphere it was but natural that he should feel the clamp placed upon him by a moderate income. He had a brother, much older than himself, and this brother was slowly dying. The brother had money, say $10,000, and it had been given out that the larger part of this money was to fall to my father. But the brother continued to linger, though his hour was surely near. Just after hearing, one day, that his brother could not survive another night, my father saw a grand opportunity to invest $5,000. The return would be quick. He would use the bank's money, and even should the investment fail, he could soon replace the amount from his brother's estate. The investment was made—and lost—and the brother grew better. In despair, father came to see me. I thought of mother and sister when I told him that I would risk everything to save him. In the express office, during the tobacco season, there was constantly a large amount of money in the company's safe. I would take $5,000 and wait for the brother to die. Well, I took that amount, and father was saved. But the brother continued to improve. And it was drawing near the time when I might expect a call from the company's inspector. I had no means of raising the money—I was not inventive—so I was forced to resort to an old trick. I blew open the safe and knocked myself senseless with an iron bar. There was money scattered all about the room when the town officer and the night watchman rushed in, and the supposition was that the robbers were too much frightened to gather it up; and when an investigation was made it was discovered that but $5,000 was missing. And the day after I was arrested the brother died. Father came heartbroken to see me the day you were put in here, and his plan was to buy off the express company, but I urged him not to attempt it, knowing that they would rather send a man to the penitentiary than to compromise for twice that amount of money. But we were agreed on one point —that no matter what was done with me the money should be mysteriously returned. Father and yourself are the only ones that know the truth. Mother and sister will always believe me innocent. I have one strong hope," he went on after a short pause, "I don't think that the doctor who examined me is overscrupulous, and, if worked skillfully, I think that we might buy him. You see I am determined to take every advantage that a thief's shrewdness can suggest. I may deserve to go to the penitentiary, but I am not enough of a Christian to suffer willingly. There, the candle's gone."

I lay down to think. I had won my fight and my reward was sure.

"What do you think of it all?" he asked when I had thought that he must be asleep.

"A sad case," I answered, pitying his frailty. The son had inherited the weakness of the father.

"And do you think that if we buy the doctor they can convict me? The fact is, I did hit myself a terrific blow."

"They will if they can," I answered.

"I know that. Good-night," he added, "I think I can sleep now."

Long before day I was up and dressed, with a few words scribbled to the Superintendent, asking to be released at once; and when the fat jailer came, I gave him the note.

During the day we talked of books, though with a lessened interest on my part.

"You don't appear to be well," he said.

"Brooding has worn my spirits away," I answered.

"But you shouldn't lose hope. Something tells me

that before long we shall be together, free and happy, ready to serve man because we have violated his laws. We will go out west where generosity gilds a fault, and live a buoyant life. And now, even if we are condemned, let us promise to join each other after our time is served. Will you promise that?"

"Yes."

"Give me your hand."

We shook hands, and he walked up and down the cell, with a smile parting his lips.

"I think more of you than any fellow I ever met, Dick. In fact, you are the only real companion I have ever known. You stimulate my mind—make me feel that I can do good in the world. I hope they won't separate us—hope that if they send us to prison they will send us together. It is awful to be companionless. Dick, you don't look well. You mustn't get sick, but if you do I'll nurse you—they mustn't take you out of here."

The fat jailer appeared. "I have a piece of news," he said. "The doctor has been called out of town for a few days, and the grand jury will skip your case, Haines, until he comes back. So you'll have a few days more of rest. Saw the foreman of the grand jury, Haines, and I told him to treat you like a blooded hoss, and if he can make up his mind to do that you are all right. But I haven't got such good news for you," he added, speaking to me; and Haines wheeled about and looked at him.

"What about me?" I asked.

"Well, they are goin' to take you over into Gasper County."

"No!" Haines cried, grasping my arm.

"That's the orders," said the jailer. "I told them that they'd better let him stay a little longer now that he'd got so well acquainted and so well liked, but they 'lowed, they did, that they believed not—said that possibly he mout come agin after the crops was laid by."

"Don't tantalize him," I cried, alarmed at the poor fellow's distress.

"Bless you, I don't want to worry him. Never want to pester a body. Well, come on."

Haines gave me his hand; his lips were trembling. He said not a word, but as I passed out he gave me a quick look and then turned his back to the door. As we were going through the corridor the jailer strove to pump me, but I shut him up and went my way.

Ah, the glory of the sunshine and the thrill of the sweet air. I stood near a garden where flowers nodded, feeling that I had been snatched from a loathsome dream. And I thought of that poor fellow who must pay for his father's greed. How harder than a rock is human justice; but he must be just or man's law becomes a laughable failure. I turned away, toward the railway station, and the sight of the express office smote me with sadness. "Poor, loyal, and generous fool," I said.

The train came. And the wheels kept repeating something—they always do. And what was it? "Remember your promise, remember your promise." Yes, I would remember it.

I had accomplished my mission and now for the reward.

The Superintendent was in his office waiting for me that evening. A check book lay in front of him.

"Ah, Captain, I am glad to see you. And what do you say?"

And instantly I replied: "The man is innocent. Turn him out."

He gave me a blank look and shoved the check book from him.

"Innocent!"

"As a lamb. Turn him out."

I stalked away, poor, but with a smile in my heart. I was a liar, but I was a man.

The money was mysteriously returned. Haines found the success lying down the road, waiting, and he found it before it had gathered rust. He is an evangelist, telling his story to the world; and his sister— she's my wife.

THE BRICK OFFICE.

In the old and remote village of Eddex stood a small brick building. Formerly it had been the law office of Judge Branham, remembered as a man of great learning and ability. And during the years that followed his death an old Justice of the Peace was wont to say, "Who will have the audacity to hang a lawyer's sign in front of the Judge's temple of wisdom?" This remark was repeated until every man in the village claimed it—the green grocer and the cobbler. Finally, it was agreed that no one should summon the senseless courage—this was the way it was put in the village—to occupy the little, dingy den once so nearly filled by the fat jurist.

The old tin sign hung there until it was blown away during a summer hail-storm, and after that the battered post stood holding out its naked arm. The property changed hands, but the office remained vacant. In the columns of the village newspaper it was offered for rent, and the young lawyers, taught to revere the great, sniffed at the announcement. But one morning the villagers were startled to see a new sign swinging from the old arm. "A. C. Jonnett, Attorney-at-law," in bright green letters, was plain to every gaze, and, of course, an insult to the memory held warmly dear.

"It is an outrage!" declared the old Justice, having hastily arrived in his shirt-sleeves. "It is intended as an insult, and ought to be pulled down. Why, I've lived in this town sixty-odd years this spring, and I never saw the like before. Hop up there, some of you, and pull off that tin blasphemy."

"Hold on," interposed the Mayor. "Let us proceed with more deliberation. Of course, this office is sacred to us, but it is now owned by a comparative stranger, and has doubtless been rented by a stranger. And, surely, when we have had a talk with him he will be willing to move to some other place. Go slow, boys. See who is inside."

A young fellow made the announcement that the office was locked.

"Ah!" said the Justice, "his conscience has smitten him and he has sneaked off. But you are right, Mr. Mayor. It is better to proceed with deliberation."

Just at that moment the tavern bell rang for breakfast. No matter what the people of a remote village may be doing, or what question the wise and ancient heads of the municipality may be discussing, the ringing of the tavern bell calls an instant halt. It is the voice announcing the crawl rather than the flight of time, and in a village the fact that one hour has succeeded another hour is a great thing to know.

The Justice and the Mayor went home to breakfast, and afterward, when they returned to renew their investigations, they found the office open. The Mayor was the first to enter; and he had advanced but a few feet beyond the threshold when he staggered back against the Justice, close upon his heels. And then the two men stood gaping in astonishment. At the desk sat a handsome young woman.

"We—we are looking for A. C. Jonnett," the Mayor stammered.

"I am that person," replied the young woman, rising, and sweetly smiling.

"What!" the Justice gasped. "You don't mean to say that you are a lawyer?"

"I don't only mean to say it, I do say it."

"But I never heard of such a thing!"

"Perhaps not; and there are doubtless many other things you never heard of."

"I don't know about that, miss. But there are a great many things I have heard of, and one of them is an honored Judge whose memory——"

"That will do," she interrupted, raising her hand. "I have heard of the Judge, and I respect his memory far more than you do. I have read his books and admire the keenness of his mind. Have you read his book on the fallacies of circumstantial evidence?"

"Didn't know he wrote one."

"I thought not. Did you wish to see me on any other business?"

"I believe not," said the Mayor. He turned toward the door, his friend moving with him, but halted, faced about, and said:

"You surely don't mean that you are going to practice law in this town?"

"Yes; that's my business."

"But the people here never heard of such a thing as a woman lawyer, and you might stay here for forty years and never get a case."

"Well, I'll try it forty years, and at the end of that time I may be able to decide whether or not to settle here permanently."

"Gosh! but you've got nerve."

And laughing at him, she replied:

"Gosh! I need it."

"I reckon you do. But," he added, giving his companion an odd wink, "even if it was common for women to practice at the bar you are too pretty for a lawyer."

"I have seen better looking criminals than lawyers," she replied, smiling.

The two men strode away. The report that the new

lawyer was a woman was spread about, and so large a crowd was soon collected about her door that the young woman closed her establishment and went to the tavern. The proprietor apologized to her for the ill-behavior of his town, and on the way to her room she halted long enough to say: " O, the novelty will wear out by the time I'm elected prosecuting attorney for this district." And the landlord, grinning as he passed on, said he reckoned it " mout " a good while before that time.

The next day was Sunday. The new lawyer went to church, to be stared at, and preached at. She sat far back toward the door, and the hemming and hawing of the minister were testimony of the annoyance he felt at beholding the honored members of his flock twisting their necks to gaze at the astounding novelty, a female barrister. She conducted herself with simple dignity, paying respectful attention to the sermon, and when the services were done she walked straightway to the hotel. About the church door a crowd gathered to discuss her, and in the midst of this idle assembly stood the old Justice of the Peace. He was more than honestly worried—he was sorely distressed. His importance had long hung upon his reminiscences of the old Judge, and by common consent he had taken charge of the great man's memory, sole executor of the estate, bonds and mortgages of recollection—and thus to be intruded upon was a fetching blow. If the intruder were only a man, come with the defiance of a man's strength, procedure would be clear; but, instead, he was confronted by a young and winsome woman. However, his duty lay before him, like a straight path, and he had but one course to pursue. He would make it so unpleasant for the woman that she would soon vacate the old office, if not the town. The Circuit Judge was his friend, and that morning they held a long conference; and now, as he stood in the middle of that idle throng, bare of his hat, with the sun beating upon his ancient head, he looked about him until his eyes fell upon the Mayor's face, and then he said:

"Speakin' in the nature of a parable, I may say that there is more ways than one of killin' a dog when you ain't got a rope to hang him with. And I want it understood that I don't mean nothin' personal, and, furthermore, that there ain't a man in all this community that's fonder of ladies' society than I am. Do you foller me?" he added, nodding at the Mayor.

"Bumpin' up agin your heels," the Mayor answered.

"I thought so. No, sir; you might git on a pert hoss and ride all day and not find a man that likes the ladies better than I do. And the fact that I have been married three times is proof of the fact. Now, I know that you gentlemen are all interested in what I'm doin', so I'll keep no secrets from you. I went over to see the Circuit Judge this mornin', and he tells me that the young woman has got the right to practice in his court, and worse than that, she can't by any due process of law be got out of the brick office; but there is a recourse. The Judge don't like the idea of a woman practicin' law, and—well, in fact, he'll make it interestin' for her from the very jump. Court opens tomorrow mornin', and I want all you gentlemen to be there."

When court assembled the next day Attorney Jonnett, duly enrolled, took her seat with the other lawyers; and when the Judge, following the usual polite custom, asked the members of the bar, one by one, if they had any motion to make, A. C. Jonnett, in a sweet voice, answered: "No motion, your Honor."

A few unimportant cases were taken up and set aside, and then work on the criminal docket was begun. The first case was that of a young man named Elliott. He had been indicted on a charge of stealing $20. He was tall, pale, nervous, with an intellectual expression of countenance. He was a stranger, had not been able to give bond, and for more than two months he had lain in jail; and now, as he had not the money wherewith to employ counsel, it was the Judge's duty to appoint a lawyer to defend him. He was guilty, of course, and such an appointment was a genial farce, but it was the law. The Judge looked about until his stern eye rested upon Attorney Jonnett. His look was interpreted, and a titter went about the room. The young woman blushed slightly, and the old Justice, nudging the Mayor, whispered :

"This here is the beginnin' of her embarrassment in this town. I like the ladies' society, understand—"

"We must have silence!" the Judge demanded: then he appointed Agnes C. Jonnett to defend the prisoner.

Now there was no red of confusion on her face. She was pale and courageous. She went over to the prisoner and sat down beside him; she went to the hotelkeeper, and shortly afterward had the defendant's bond fixed. She announced that the defense was not ready for trial, and was given three days for preparation. During that time she worked day and night, and when the case was called she was ready. Her examination of the witnesses was sharp, and the prosecuting attorney gave her many a look of antagonistic admiration. Finally, the argument was begun, and then she surprised the court. Her command of language was exquisite; she was impassioned, and upon a backwoods jury passion falls with the grace of a gospel. She wrung tears from the eyes of those rough but softhearted men; she threw upon them a hypnotic spell of pathos; she convinced them that the young man was innocent, and a verdict of not guilty was brought in.

The tavern bell was ringing as she left the courtroom. Some one spoke to her. She looked up and recognized the old Justice.

"Miss, I reckon I am about as good a critic as you'd find in a day's ride—mout ride a pert hoss from sun to sun and not find a keener one—and I want to say that you made as good a speech as I ever heard."

"I thank you, sir."

"O, not at all. You proved that young fellow's innocence beyond a doubt; and he can settle right down and live here if he wants to."

"I am glad to hear you say that," she replied, walking along with him. "At first I thought him guilty, but now I know he is not. And, by the way, he is going to settle down here. He is a doctor."

"You don't say so? He didn't look it. But when a man gets down in the world, and lays in jail awhile, he don't look much of anything. Fust thing we knowed of him he was pokin' round here like he was sorter daft. By the way," he added, halting at the corner of the street, "I want to tell you not to give yourself no uneasiness about that brick office. You may stay there as long as you want to. I've done my duty by the old Judge, and that's all anybody can do."

Elliott began the practice of medicine. He had been graduated from a well-known institution, and was really a skillful physician. But concerning himself he was strangely silent. One day he successfully performed a startling surgical operation and the countryside rang with his name. Every day his buggy was stopped in front of the little brick office, and a smile always welcomed him. He called one night when Agnes was late at work. That day his buggy had not stopped, and laughingly he said he had called to explain.

"Look here," he broke out, taking a seat near her desk, "do you know that this is our anniversary?"

"Our anniversary? What do you mean?"

"One year ago to-day you saved me from prison."

"O!" was all she said, looking down.

"And now, looking back, it seems that I never lived until then—I was born that day, for with your smile came the sweet breath of life."

"Flatterer!" she said.

"No, a rare example—gratitude." She looked at him, and in her glance was a thrilling question. "More than gratitude," he hastened to say.

"What can be more than gratitude?"

"Love," he answered.

*　*　*　*　*　*　*　*

A soft wind came out of the woods, and the tin sign swung on the old arm of the post. They stood by the desk, and his arm was about her. Suddenly he took it away, stepped back, and folded his arms.

"Agnes, I have made a sweet confession, and now I must make a bitter one. I was guilty."

"What?" she cried, drawing back.

"Listen to me. I stole the $20. I came here a vagabond, not knowing whither I went—a victim of morphine. I was moneyless. All night I raved. I thought I should go mad; I was mad, and at morning I stole the money and ran away to get the drug. I got it, and then the awful sense of my crime came upon me, and when they found me I was in a fence corner praying, with my mother's voice throbbing in my ears. They took me to jail, and there, with the determination of one inspired, I lessened my allowance of morphine until I cured myself. Yes, I cured my body, and in the sight of God you cured my soul. Long ago I refunded three times the amount of the theft—sent it anonymously. And now, Agnes——"

She held out her hands to him.

THE GREEK GOD BARBER.

Bocage and a friend went into a barber shop, and when they came out, Bocage remarked: "Those barbers in there are about as distinguished looking a set of fellows as I ever saw. The one that shaved you might easily be taken for a United States Senator, while the one who condescended to accommodate me could serve as a faultless model for a Greek god. I think that if I had a jury composed of such material, I could make a speech that would charm back to rosy life the long cold and dusty ear of Cicero."

"Bocage," said the friend, "for a man who hopes to make his living by the laying down of dull law, you are the silliest sentimentalist I have ever seen. I laid a wager some time ago that a sudden outcropping of this trait would one day get you in trouble. You can't go even into a barber shop, the place, perhaps, for sarcasm, but never for sentiment, without having your fancy aroused."

"Perhaps I should have been a poet," Bocage answered, dodging a cab.

"But don't you think that selling flowers instead of

trying to give them voice, lies closer to the scope of your abilities?"

"That's all right, old fellow, you may guy me as much as you please, but you can not alter the fact that the man who shaved me looks like a Greek god; and how easy it would be for him, although he may be as ignorant as a guinea-pig, to go to some fashionable watering place and pass himself off as a distinguished personage, marry the handsomest girl in the country. Well, I must leave you here."

"Going out of town, are you?"

"Yes, going to Lake Minnetonka for a few weeks."

* * * * * *

The evening was charming. The air was as soft as a whispered sentiment. Music, refined into an echo, floated across the lake; well-dressed men and fashionable women promenaded on the long veranda of a summer hotel. Bocage had smoked himself into sentimental listlessness and was sitting apart from the slowly moving throng. Suddenly he became wide awake. A beautiful girl, on the arm of a Greek god model, passed him.

"There's my barber," he said to himself. "I will watch him, and when the proper time comes, I will send him back to his shop. I have been here two weeks and no one has paid any particular attention to me, but here comes a barber and becomes at once a champion of beauty. I will follow the fellow."

He followed along with well-disguised aimlessness, until he met the proprietor of the hotel. "Captain," said he, "who is that nice looking man walking with that beautiful girl?"

The captain, after looking a moment, asked, "Do you mean that tall, young fellow and blondish girl?

"Yes."

"Why, he is a Mr. Stockbridge, of Lexington, Kentucky, and she is Miss Ambridge, of Baltimore."

"I wonder if they have known each other long."

"That I can't say. I believe, however, that they met for the first time several nights ago."

"I should like to be presented."

"Well, that can be arranged easily enough. Yonder is her father. I'll introduce you to him."

Bocage was presented to Mr. Ambridge, and found him to be an exceedingly pleasant old gentleman, with a remarkably unworldly air.

"May I ask what business you are engaged in?" Bocage asked.

"Your question is perfectly proper," said the old gentleman, noticing that his new acquaintance was slightly embarrassed. "I am not really in any business, being the rector of one of the leading churches of our city. I have come hither for rest, having done much labor of late. This is my first visit to this delightful spot, having hitherto spent my vacations at the seaside."

"Did you come alone?"

"No, my daughter is with me. She has just returned from Rome, whither she went to study art; not that she purposes to follow painting as a means of livelihood, but to indulge the longing of the purest of all sentiment. She is coming now."

"That—er—excuse me—but that handsome lady with the tall young man?"

"Yes."

"A friend of the family, I suppose."

"Well, no. A comparatively new acquaintance."

"I should like to be presented. Of course, I am a stranger to you, but the proprietor of this hotel, a man, as you doubtless know, of eminent respectability, will vouch for my standing."

Bocage was presented; the barber scanned him closely. Bocage felt the blood of triumph surging through his veins. He would let the fellow play awhile, and then he would reel him in. After dinner Bocage sought Stockbridge and asked him if he would not take a stroll. Stockbridge hesitated a moment and then said that he would. They walked along the beach.

"Where are you from, Mr. Stockbridge?"

"Kentucky."

"Have you lived there long?"

"I was born there, but I have been away so much that I know but little of the State."

"Foreign travel?" Bocage asked.

Stockbridge hesitated a moment, and then replied:

"No, not exactly, although I have been in Mexico a good deal."

"You are pretty well acquainted with our own country, I should think."

"Well, no, I can't say that I am."

"You have been in Chicago, I presume."

"Why do you presume so?"

"Oh, I don't know, except that nearly every American visits Chicago sooner or later."

"I have been in Chicago."

"Yes, I'll bet you have," Bocage mused.

"But it is too rushing for my nerves," Stockbridge continued.

"Yes, it is rushing, but it has many advantages over a quieter place. Our hotels are great, and it is said that our barber shops can't be beaten."

"Suppose we return to the hotel," said Stockbridge. "I have an engagement."

They returned to the hotel. Bocage went to his room, and when he came down he saw the barber and Miss Ambridge sitting on the veranda. He joined them, expressing a hope that he did not intrude.

"Oh, not in the least," said the young lady. "I have just been trying to convince Mr. Stockbridge that he ought to read Arnold's 'Light of the World,' and I trust that you will come to my assistance."

"As a man of taste, he should read that great work," Bocage answered. He had never read it—had merely glanced at its skeleton printed in a newspaper. "I am very fond of it," he continued, "and think that it is really better than the 'Light of Asia.'"

"I can hardly agree with you there," said Miss Ambridge. "The 'Light of Asia' being more paganish is, to my mind, more poetic. Christianity has not improved poetry, although it has blessed the world. Poetry, in its truest and sublimest sense, is the light of the dawn, and not the glare of noontide. Do you agree with me, Mr. Stockbridge?"

"Well, I don't know much about it; to tell you the truth, I never read much poetry, except in the newspapers. I like a good book, such as 'Allen Quartermain.'"

"Oh, no," cried the girl; "say 'Lorna Doone.'"

"I never read that."

"Then you have missed the sweetest novel in the English language," said Bocage, who had struggled up to the great snow-storm and had then put down the book and taken up "She."

"Well, I don't know about that," Stockbridge replied. ",I reckon a man reads the books that suit him best, and I guess his taste in reading is pretty much the same as it is in music. He likes what he does like and that's about all there is to it."

"You are right," said Bocage. "Take opera, for instance. Some people like one opera and some another. One man will go into ecstasies over 'Otello,' while another is perfectly satisfied with the 'Barber of Seville.'"

"Will you please excuse me a moment?" Stockbridge asked, rising.

"Yes," said the girl; "but you won't stay long, will you?"

"No, not long."

"Isn't he grand and delightful?" she remarked, when the barber, not of Seville, but of Chicago, had withdrawn.

"Yes," said Bocage, "he is a very nice-looking man; rather neat, too."

"Neat doesn't express it," the girl replied, "he is so noble-looking."

"What business is he engaged in?"

"Well, I don't know that he is in any business, but his father is the owner of a fine blue-grass farm and has many blooded horses, I understand."

"Did he say so?"

"Yes, or I should not have known it."

"Humph," Bocage grunted.

"But do you doubt it, Mr. Bocage?"

"Suppose I should say that I have reason for doubting it?"

"Oh, but I don't see how you can have reason for saying so. He has conducted himself as a perfect gentleman ever since I met him and I have no cause for doubting his word."

"He has conducted himself as a gentleman so far as I know, and yet I have cause to doubt his word. Now, I am going to say something for your own good. I saw you with that man and I was at once interested in your behalf and was determined to warn you. Mind you, I shall say nothing against the man's calling, for it is a necessary one, but I despise his pretense. He is simply a Chicago barber."

"Oh, Mr. Bocage, you ought to be ashamed of yourself."

"I am telling the truth. He works in a Dearborn street shop and shaved me the day I left Chicago. He's coming back. I must bid you good-night."

The next morning when Bocage came down, Stockbridge was waiting for him. "Let me see you a moment," said the barber.

"Am I next?" Bocage sarcastically asked.

"You are next so far as I am concerned. What

have you been telling Miss Ambridge about me?" Stockbridge asked, drawing Bocage aside.

"I suppose you know."

"Yes, I know, for she told me. You say that I am a Chicago barber."

"And I acknowledge that you are a good one. I don't care how much you enjoy yourself or how high you aspire, but I despise pretense. If you had come here without any disguise, I should have—well, I haven't time to talk to you."

"But I have time to talk and to act unless you make proper amends. You must go to that young lady and tell her that you are a liar."

"Mind how you talk, or I shall not be responsible for my action. Tell her that I am a liar, indeed, when I couldn't even tell her that I was mistaken. You know, as well as you know anything, that you shaved me not long ago."

"I will give you until noon to apologize to that lady."

"Why apologize to her? I have said nothing about her."

"No matter, you have slandered her future husband."

"Now, look here," said Bocage, "you can't bluff me. I won't have it. If the girl is a mind to marry you after what I have said, all right."

"Even if I had shaved you——"

"Which you did."

"Well, then, don't you think that you have acted the part of a coward?"

"No, I think I have acted the part of a man in exposing a fellow who is seeking to deceive a trusting girl."

"All right. Do you think, though, that you will be ready by noon to acknowledge to Miss Ambridge that you are a liar?"

"I am as ready now as I shall ever be."

"I will give you until noon."

"By noon," said Bocage, as he strode off, "he will be gone. I rather like his gall. Why, helloa, judge!" he suddenly exclaimed, springing forward and seizing the hand of an elderly-looking gentleman. "When did you arrive?"

"Just now."

"How's everything in Louisville?"

"Oh, moving along smoothly. I am looking for Louis Stockbridge, of Lexington."

"Ah, have you met him?"

"Not since I came here, but I have known him a long time—his father is an old friend of mine."

"Can it be possible!" Bocage exclaimed.

"It must be possible when it is already a fact. What do you mean?"

"Why, sir, I took that man Stockbridge to be a Chicago barber."

"You'd better not tell him so."

"But I have told him so and he has given me until noon to apologize to—to—the young lady. It is all mixed up."

"Well, then, you'd better straighten it out by making the amplest apology within the range of retraction's most persuasive language."

"I must be a fool. By George! I would have sworn that he was a barber. Yonder he comes. I don't like to apologize here, unless I can do it quietly. There are too many people looking."

Stockbridge and the judge cordially greeted each other and then Bocage stepped up. "My dear sir," said he, "I have made an egregious blunder——"

"I think so," replied Stockbridge, "and I have decided not to give you until noon," and, wheeling Bocage about, he kicked him off the veranda.

*   *   *   *   *   *

The next day while Bocage was walking along Dearborn street, he glanced into a barber shop and saw a man that looked like a Greek god rubbing the swollen head of a drunken Swede.

UGLY RACHEL.

In the Cumberland mountains, near a much-traveled road, and not far from a stream that seemed to exist in a succession of accidental tumblings, there once lived an old man who held natural claims to local distinction, but who was chiefly known for one cause. He was a wonderful rifle shot, but this brought him no fame; he was one of the most skillful of fishermen, but this aroused not the slightest degree of interest; he was a dangerous opponent in a wrestle; a champion at a corn-shucking; a notably solemn man at a funeral; a marked rejoicer at a celebration; an astonishing breaker of colts; a master of stubborn steers, and the terror of balky horses, and yet all these accomplishments, any two of which are quite enough to bring renown to a man in almost any mountain community, were disregarded. Why, then, was he known to all? Simply because he was the father of Rachel Moss. It had often been declared by men of keen judgment and women of unerring taste, that Rachel was the most unattractive, indeed, the ugliest girl that nature could possibly form. She had the hayest-like hair, the catist-like eyes that had ever been seen; her mouth looked like an incision made in impulsive revenge, and her chin was the very climax of ill-shape. No imagination could picture a more unattractive woman.

Naturally enough, Rachel was never invited into "society." No one seemed to think that there could possibly be any enjoyment for her. Once a young fellow, who, in early youth had been struck on the head with a stone and who had afterward been nearly squeezed to death by a bear, a man who, in short, was a jabbering idiot, chattered a declaration of love to her, and every one who heard of it roared with laughter.

Old man Moss, Rachel's father, took summer boarders, but the girl never attempted to force her presence upon them. When not engaged in the kitchen, or when not shyly picking her way along the tumbling stream, she sat alone in an attic room.

One evening a distinguished looking traveler stopped at the old Moss house. He was an artist and at one time had dreamed of fame, but the unexpected inheritance of a large estate and the ease which naturally followed, turned his mind from the thoughts of a struggle for a place in the capricious world of art. He had passed through seasons of dissipation and was now seeking rest far from the exacting eye of fashion. He paid no attention to the other boarders—he lived within himself. The days passed, and although he politely answered every question addressed to him, he avoided meeting any one. After a time he was put down as a man suffering from the gnawings of remorse

One day he caught the sight of Rachel. His first impression was a shudder of repulsion, and then moved by a strange fascination, he sought a better view of her face, which, when gained, made him yearn to get a closer look at her features. The dinner hour was over and the boarders sat in the shade of the porch, nodding. The woodpecker, with his red head glaring in the sunlight, tapped on the dead arm of a white oak tree, and a ragged sheep, with her eyes bulging in a melancholy stare, stood in the dusty road. Rachel slyly stole away, and sought the cool brink of the hurrying stream. The artist followed her. She had gone some distance up the rugged glade, and, pausing under an over-cup acorn tree, was looking at a wild honeysuckle that trembled under the weight of a humming-bird, when she heard a stone splash in the water. The next moment she had turned to run away, when the artist scrambled out of the stream, whither a treacherous bowlder had thrown him and cried:

"Please wait a moment."

She paused, though with painful embarrassment, until he approached, and, half hiding her face, waited for him to speak.

"If the water had been deeper I should have had a good ducking," said he. "I am not as dry as a powder-horn, as it is."

"I am sorry you fell in," she answered.

"Oh, it doesn't amount to anything," he cheerfully replied. "We live in the same house, I believe?" he continued after a pause.

"Yes, I am Mr. Moss' daughter."

"I didn't know he had a daughter."

"Then you have not heard of me?"

"No, I have heard of nothing concerning the family affairs of any one in this neighborhood."

"You have been fortunate," she said, with the merest suggestion of bitterness in the tone of her voice. "I didn't suppose that any one could escape hearing an account of my father's unfortunate celebrity."

"I don't comprehend your meaning," he rejoined. "Is your father celebrated on account of a misfortune?"

"Yes."

"And may I ask what that misfortune is?"

"The fact that he is my father," she answered.

"But why is that a misfortune?"

"Can't you see?" she bitterly asked, throwing aside, with unwonted boldness, her old sun bonnet, and exposing every feature of her face. "Don't you see that it is because I am unrivalled in my ugliness?

Come, be honest enough to acknowledge that you do see."

"I confess that you may be without a rival in your unenvied line of distinction, but I can't see why the old man should be held accountable."

"Oh, your honesty is charming," she cried, laughing merrily; "I never encountered such frankness outside a book."

"You know something of books, then, do you?"

"Yes, I have been driven into an acquaintance with them. You must know that among ignorant people much depends upon looks. Intelligence counts for nothing, and cultivation is looked upon as a weakness or rather as an insanity. An old school teacher boarded at our house years ago, and filled our attic— now my attic—with books. He was kind enough, or tolerant enough, to teach me, and when he died, he left me his books. That is, he was unable to take them with him, and as no one else wanted them they became my property. If I had been passably good looking, I should doubtless have never looked into them, but as my face was my physical misfortune I was driven to the attic for my only real pleasure. I know but little of the neighborhood gossip, and, therefore, have but little to say to the neighbors. In fact, I am ashamed to talk to ignorant people."

"I must thank you for the compliment you are now paying me," said the artist.

"Oh, you are under no obligations whatever. But to tell you the truth I am surprised that I should talk so freely to you, a total stranger. I suppose, though, we all have our moods. If I had seen you sooner, I should have run away."

"I'm glad you didn't, for I am in need of your society, although I am not so very bookish. I have devoted my life to the study of art."

"There you have a decided advantage of me," she answered. "I know nothing whatever of art, except what I have read."

"In that event you know as much as most people, for there are thousands of pretended art critics who do not even read about it. By the way, I have become interested in you."

"Thank you. I will attempt to make better bread after this."

"I am serious," he earnestly declared.

"So am I," she replied. "There is nothing more serious than making bread."

"Come, now, don't guy me; don't make fun of me."

"I don't think I can make anything of you more than you are."

"That's a compliment, or it isn't, I don't know

which; but, really, I am interested in you and have a favor to ask."

"What is it?"

"That you will meet me here every day."

"But I should like to know why."

"I can't tell you now—I will some other time."

"I can't promise."

"But will you meet me here to-morrow?"

"Yes, I will promise that, but I don't know why. Indeed, if I had been told an hour ago that I should ever have agreed to meet any one, and especially a man, I—well, I could not have thought such a thing possible. I must go now."

The artist sat for a time gazing after her and then he gave himself up to meditation. He was interested in her—more deeply interested than he had ever been in any human being. "I will paint her portrait," he had mused while talking to her. "From the very childhood of art down to its unrevered gray hairs to-day, the artist has sought in high and low life, the beautiful face that should on his canvas, carry his name down through 'all time to come.' Why should not I reverse this order—why should not those ugly features bear my name to generations yet to come? I will win her consent and will paint a true portrait, which, in comparison, shall show 'Medusa' as a joy for ever, being so truly a thing of beauty."

He sat there deeply meditating, and to him there came back, as if an anxious hour of the necessitous past had stepped into the prosperous and easy present, a dream of fame, a dream so vivid and intense that he shook with agitation.

The next day he was sitting on that same rock, when Rachel came. "I don't know why I am so prompt," she said. "In fact, I don't know why I have come at all, yet something seemed to be drawing me."

His blood leaped. Fate herself was aiding him. "I should have been greatly disappointed if you hadn't come," he answered. "Isn't the day lovely?"

"Yes, it falls upon the earth like God's beneficent smile." He looked up quickly, and wished that he could have thrown her face upon the canvas at that moment. He asked her to name her favorite books, and for more than an hour he sat listening to the passionate praise which she bestowed upon her friends, and at times he fancied himself attempting to paint her words. Once he thought to tell her of the intended portrait, but discretion whispered that the time was not yet in full bloom.

Day after day they met under the over-cup acorn tree. The time was in full bloom and he said: "Rachel, I have another great favor to ask of you, the greatest that I could possibly ask."

"Is it that I might still farther improve in my bread making?"

"Will you never forbear to ridicule me? What do I care for bread? Bread may be the staff of life, but art is the wing of the soul. I want to paint a portrait of you; want to paint you just as you are, so that in after years I can look upon your face and bring up these surroundings."

She laughed. He looked up in surprise. "A miracle has been wrought," she said. "A man has cultivated me for my face alone. Yes, you may paint my picture, for your poorest work can but flatter me; but I shall name the conditions. The picture must be painted here, and at no time must you work on it after I have told you to stop."

"The conditions are satisfactory, Rachel. I will begin to-morrow."

Day after day she sat for him. Sometimes, with his brush just ready to touch the canvas, he would pause and listen to her as if her words were the unexpected wild-wood notes, and sometimes, when she seemed to be inspired with poetry, he would turn away from his work and in a tranquil rapture gaze upon her. One day he touched the canvas and, throwing down his brush, exclaimed:

"God in Heaven, it is beautiful." It was the picture of a divine face—the features of an angel. "Rachel," he cried, "I have painted your soul. See," it sprang from the canvas like a burst of light. "Look, girl, I have caught a face fresh from Heaven's mould. It is your soul, girl, it is your soul! Look, Rachel!" He ran to her and started back in horror. She was lifeless, and his brush had caught the image of her passing soul.

THE MOON IN THE PICTURE.

CHARACTERS.

John Radfield, general inspector American Express Company; Harvey Gray, a handsome deaf mute; Nick Bowles, a detective; Nat Morris, son of widow; Jerry, colored man of all work; Widow Morris; Laura, pretty daughter of widow; Harriet, old maid daughter of widow.

ACT I.

TIME, THE PRESENT.

SCENE—*Farm house of widow, turned into summer resort, Northern Illinois. Parlor, plainly furnished, old melodeon or piano, center table, sofa, rocking chairs, several upholstered chairs, simple pictures on wall, door C, small mirror on wall L, blind fireplace L covered with screen, poker decorated with a ribbon leaning against wall near screen. Curtain rises discovering Laura sitting on sofa; Jerry, with hat wadded in his hand, standing near the door as if about to go out.*

JERRY—An' ez I wus sayin' ter myse'f, ef dat man Mr. Radfield has got so much money, w'y doan he go ober yander ter de hotel dat da built 'cross de lake?

Ef I had money like da say he has, you wouldn't see me roostin' on de groun'; huh, see me up in de highest tree. But I doan know whuther he got money or not; he ain't come showin' me none.

LAURA—(*smiling*) People don't usually go round showing their money.

JERRY—(*jolting himself with a laugh*) *He* doan, an' dat's er fack. But whut's de matter wid dat uder generman?

LAURA—Who, Mr. Gray? Why, he is a deaf mute.

JERRY—Huh, an' I reckon dat's de reason he kain't talk. Now ain't dat er mighty bad fix fur er person ter be in? 'Pear ter me like ef I couldn't talk I'd jest hatter—hatter—talk anyhow; jest couldn't keep from it. Dar ain't nuthin' dat could keep me frum it, I tell you, caze when I gits mad it—it—it jest talks itse'f. Wall, I must be gwine now. I clar I so busy I doan know what ter do fust. An' do you know dat yo' sister come er callin' me lazy? Yas, she did. Come woke me up whar I wuz lyin' er sleep out dar under er apple tree jest ter call me lazy. Dat wan't no way ter act, an' says I, "gone way frum yere, chile, an' doan fool wid me caze I'se dangus." Yas, I mus' go, now.

LAURA—Well, why don't you go on?

JERRY—Who, me? Now you ain't goin' ter turn er gin me, is you? I neber seed sich times ez dese yere.

Eber body tellin' you ter go on now. An' I'm gwine, too. Wall, I must go. Whut you want ter keep holdin' me yere fur?

LAURA—(*with pretended anger*) You trifling rascal, I'm not holding you. Go on.

JERRY—Dat's whut I said I gwine do. Yere I goes. (*Exit.*)

Enter HARVEY GRAY.

LAURA—What a pity it is that he can neither hear nor talk. (*Gray takes the rocking chair and turning it toward her, sits down.*) Yes, and he is so handsome, too. How sad he looks. They say that it is just as much as he can do to write his name. What a pity. (*Suddenly brightening*) But what a chance this is for me to say what I please to a man. And, oh, how I can practice on him and say lovely things to him. Oh, how handsome you are; and I am in love with you. Now, sir, what do you think of that? Why don't you tell me how delightful it is to have a modest girl tell you of her love? Poor man, I am sorry for you, and I'm going to keep on telling you how much I love you. You are just as sweet as you can be. Why, he's not even looking at me. Never mind, sir. You don't appreciate your good fortune; you don't know what a precious thing a young girl's love is; and a handsome girl, too. (*Springs from the sofa and humorously poses in front of mirror.*) Now you may think that this is vanity, but if you do, you won't say anything about it, will you? You mustn't because you are my sweetheart, you know.

Enter MISS HARRIET.

HARRIET—Why, whom are you talking to?

LAURA—Oh, to Mr. Gray.

HARRIET—What a silly goose you are.

LAURA—Why, just because I have taken advantage of the opportunity to say what I please to a man? I can't let such a privilege slip past me. (*Takes hold of Harriet and attempts to waltz with her.*)

HARRIET—(*freeing herself*) For gracious sake stop your foolishness. I never saw such a girl. What must this man think of you, cutting up this way?

LAURA—It doesn't make any difference what he thinks. He won't say anything about it, will you precious? (*to Gray.*)

HARRIET—(*with energy*) Laura, I'm ashamed of you. Go on out there and help mother set the table.

LAURA—(*with mock concern*) And will you promise not to make love to my sweetheart while I'm gone?

HARRIET—(*laughing in spite of all efforts at restraint*) Oh, go on with you. You are enough to make a cat laugh.

LAURA—(*with assumed surprise*) And I have

tickled my sister, and my only sister at that. (*Hums a tune, waltzes, exit.*)

HARRIET—(*taking up a book and seating herself on the sofa*) I wonder how much longer Mr. Radfield is going to stay. He is in love with Laura and she is a fool if she doesn't marry him. They would live in the city and I could spend the most of my time with them. He likes me; I can see that.

The door is partly open. Radfield looks in.

HARRIET—(*Moving over to one end of the sofa*) Come in.

RADFIELD—(*entering with dignity and taking a chair, turns his back on Gray, who dreamily sits there, slowly rocking*) Rather warm in the sun. (*Looks toward the door and perceiving the widow Morris,*) Why don't you come in and rest a while, madam? You are simply working yourself to death.

WIDOW—(*entering, seating herself on the sofa beside Harriet and fanning herself*) A body does have to scuffle mightily to make a living these days, I tell you. Up this morning by daylight and have been going it ever since.

RADFIELD—(*bowing*) Pardon me if I obtrude a suggestion, but why don't you insist upon your daughters——

HARRIET—Now, Mr. Radfield, you needn't say that we don't help her. Oh, I know what you were going to say (*shaking her finger at him*), and you needn't say it. Mama knows that we help her all the time.

Radfield—(*apologetically*) Yes, I suppose you do. I was merely joking. But it is a shame that a woman must work so hard.

Widow—(*still fanning herself*) Well, I'm glad that there's one man who looks at it that way. They are precious few, goodness knows, and if I were a girl I would not marry a man until he acknowledged—acknowledged—well, you know what I mean. I have so many ideas but haven't the language to express them with.

Radfield—But you have language enough to discharge that lazy negro. Why don't you fire him?

Widow—I can't for he did us a great service once, not very long ago. My son Nat fell into the lake and Jerry saved him from drowning, and I can't discharge him on that account and ——

Radfield—(*in an undertone*) Rather a doubtful service.

Widow—(*looking inquiringly at him*) What did you say, sir?

Radfield—I said it was a great service.

Widow—Oh, yes indeed, for I don't know what we should do without dear Nat. He is such a good ——

(*A voice without crying,* Maw, oh, maw.)

Widow—What is it, my son?

Nat—*(appearing at door)* Make Laura gimmy my knife.

Widow—Laura, dear, give him his knife.

Laura—*(without)* Haven't seen his knife.

Nat—She has, too. First thing she knows I'll whip her, too. All time tryin' to run over me. *(Enters with his fists doubled, and approaches his mother. She reaches up and puts his hair back out of his eyes.)*

Widow—Can't you speak to Mr. Radfield?

Nat—Don't want to speak to him; ain't got nothin' to tell him.

Widow—Well, go on out now, and split some stove wood.

Nat—Make Jerry split it.

Jerry—*(thrusting his head in at the door)* Whut's dat? Boy, you doan know whut you talkin' bout. I—I—I split wood befo you wuz born, chile.

Radfield—And you haven't split any since, have you?

Jerry—*(with great indignation)* Look yere, white pusson, ain't you 'feard dat mouth o' yourn will go off some time an' hurt you?

Widow—*(with anger)* Jerry, you impudent rascal, get away from that door! Get away this instant.

Jerry—*(looking up and down the door)* Ain't hurt de do'. Lemme see, did I knock a splinter off yere? No, de do' is all right.

THE MOON IN THE PICTURE.

Harriet—Mr. Radfield, what was that you were telling me yesterday about the moon in the picture?

Radfield—Oh, I was simply telling you about a piece of perfect art. A friend of mine was suddenly stricken with insomnia; he tried all sorts of remedies, but couldn't sleep. He consulted numerous doctors, but they were unable to do anything for him. He had been a sound sleeper, and the sudden loss of this faculty not only frightened him but puzzled him as well. And finally the cause came out: He had bought a picture and had hung it in his bedroom, and in the picture was a moon, and the moon, being full, shone in his face and robbed him of sleep.

Jerry—Well, (*scratching his head*) I has been on han' at er good many stretches o' de truth, but dis yere is er bout de stretchest stretch I eber seed. De moon in de pictur', er haw! haw! (*Disappears.*)

Widow—(*to Nat*) Go on now and wash your face for dinner.

Nat—(*frowning*) All time have to wah—wash my face. Washed it yesterday.

Radfield—I didn't suppose it had been wet since you fell into the lake.

Nat—(*moving toward the door*) Want you to let me alone, now. All time tryin' to run over me. Laura! (*calling loudly*) want my knife. Goin' to hurt you first thing you know, too. Tell this feller that you are in love with him the first thing you know (*looking at Radfield.*) All time taking my knife. (*Exit.*)

WIDOW—(*arising*) Well, I must see about dinner.

HARRIET—Want me to help you, mama?

WIDOW—No; there's but little to do now. (*Exit.*)

HARRIET—(*appearing to be much relieved*) When you want me to do anything call me.

Gray arises as if from a doze, walks about the room, looks at the pictures, goes back to the rocking chair, places his hand upon the back of it as if meditating, and suddenly turning leaves the room.

HARRIET—Poor man, what a pity.

RADFIELD—Oh, I don't know about that. He misses hearing a great many disagreeable things.

HARRIET—But he also misses music, which is the greatest of misfortunes.

RADFIELD—Yes, and he fails to hear the bagpipes when the Scotch have a picnic, and that is a blessing.

HARRIET—What a funny man you are, Mr. Radfield. (*Suddenly as if moved by an inspiration*) But he hears no word of love, and missing that, life has gone to seed without having bloomed.

RADFIELD—Good, that is, in a poetic way, but he also hears no word of hate and therefore misses the bitterness of the human heart. It is but natural, however, you should turn to the poetry of nature, living as you do in the very whisper of nature's secrets; to you there is a sigh in the wind, a tear in the cloud, a smile in the rays of the sun; but to people who live in the actual world, the hard, grinding world, there is so much bald necessity that there can be but little beauty, little of the poetry of sweet inference. There, the pleasant man may be the scoundrel and the uncouth and hated person may be the real gentleman. It is only on the stage that the villain wears his principles stamped upon his countenance.

LAURA—(*calling from without*) Mr. Radfield, there's a man out here that wants to see you.

RADFIELD—Tell him to come in.

Enter Nick Bowels. Bows to Radfield, and then looks toward Harriet.

HARRIET—(*arising*) I will go and help mother with the dinner. (*Exit.*)

BOWLES—(*Seating himself and leaning toward Radfield*) Well, sir, I am here.

RADFIELD—So I see. Now I suppose you thoroughly understand the case. The robbery of the express office at Mingago occurred about six months ago. The first thing the agent knew, one night, he saw a man in the room, and the next thing he knew he was lying stunned on the floor. Some $20,000 were taken out, money that had been forwarded a few days before and was consigned to a party of men who had made rather large purchases of land. We put some of the very best detectives at work on the case, and one by one they were withdrawn. There is a reward of $5,000 offered, and—well, I have discovered a clue. Wait a moment. (*Detective leaning eagerly toward him*) Yes, I have a clue. I came up here to spend a short vacation, simply because I am tired of large resorts and hotels, and I have improved my time. In this house is a deaf and dumb fellow named Gray. He is the robber.

Bowles—How do you know?

Radfield—Oh, I don't know for certain, but I believe it. I have discovered, no matter how, that the work was done by a deaf mute. And why? He was acting with a gang who wanted an agent that could not well inform on them. As I say, I am not absolutely certain, but a few days more will absolutely settle it. Now you stay about here, and when I give you the word, nab him.

Bowles—But you must be reasonably sure. It is dangerous to snatch up a man——

Radfield—Don't you worry; I'll fix that.

Laura—(*laughing and thrusting her head in at the door*) Come on to dinner.

Curtain.

Act II.

ONE WEEK LATER.

SCENE—*Same. Gray and Laura entering room as curtain goes up. Gray takes rocking chair; Laura flounces about on sofa and then settles herself at one end of it.*

LAURA—And we had such a delightful time in the boat, didn't we sweetheart? Why, I didn't know you could row so well. Why didn't you tell me? But you don't tell everything you know, do you? My, I'm not half so discreet as you are. I tell everything I know and would tell more if I could think of it. And you haven't told me how long you intend to stay. Humph, you haven't told me yet where you live. Ain't it funny to be in love with a man and not know where he lives? You are just too sweet for anything. Who would have ever thought that I could talk this way to a man? But it won't go any farther, will it sweetheart? Oh, but how are you going to ask mama for my hand, you sweet thing? But I must quit this foolishness. The first thing I know I shall be in love with you sure enough. I declare I have felt so sorry for you that I believe I am actually in love with you. Yes, and I can love you all I want to and nobody will be the wiser. Isn't it nice to make a doll of a man? And suppose I get mad, I can scold you all I please and you would never say a word. How nice of you that would be. You are surely an exception. Why, my papa before he died used to scold mama every once in a while. What am I talking about? Of course he couldn't scold her after he died. (*Gets up and walks about the room. Poses in front of the mirror. Hums a tune and waltzes. Gray smiles and nods his head.*) You like that, don't you sweetheart? And your smile isn't dumb, is it? No, indeed, for it tells me a great deal. (*Gray smiles and nods his head.*) Yes, it does, you sweet thing.

Enter RADFIELD.

RADFIELD—(*Drawing a chair to the center table, sitting down with one arm carelessly on table*) Well, I see that you are alone.

LAURA—(*surprised*) Alone! Why, no; Mr. Gray is with me.

RADFIELD—So I see, but unfortunately he is no company.

LAURA—Quite as good company as some people who talk more but who really say less.

RADFIELD—(*softly laughing*) You believe then in the wisdom of silence.

LAURA—The poets have said that the sweetest music makes no sound.

RADFIELD—And the poets have talked nonsense.

LAURA—Not when they were silent.

RADFIELD—Good. Did you enjoy your boat ride?

LAURA—(*with enthusiasm*) It was delightful.

RADFIELD—And I want you to go with me some time.

LAURA—(*spiritedly*) Oh, you want me to go with you. Is that the way to ask?

RADFIELD—(*bowing*) I should have said that I desire that pleasure.

LAURA—Oh, that's different. But I can't go with you; I'm engaged for the season.

RADFIELD—Not to dummy, I hope.

LAURA—(*angrily*) Mr. Radfield, you should not speak that way. This man can't help his affliction. I won't talk to you (*Arising.*)

RADFIELD—(*apologetically*) Pardon me, please. Wait just a moment. Wait, please, I was joking. (*Laura halts near the door.*) I have something to say to you.

LAURA—Well, say it.

RADFIELD—Sit down and I will.

LAURA—No, I'll stand here.

RADFIELD—I hardly know how to begin.

LAURA—Then what you were going to say must not be very important.

RADFIELD—Yes, it is of great importance, and that is the reason I don't know how to begin.

LAURA—Well, I'm waiting.

RADFIELD—(*seriously*) Miss Laura—

LAURA—That's a good start.

Radfield—Miss Laura, I have thought—

Laura—Oh, you *have* thought. You surprise me.

Radfield—Please give me time. I have thought since coming here that I had found the most charming spot on the face of the earth; and the secret of that charm has made itself known to me. I love you. Please wait. Yes, I love you. I know how awkward this confession is, for I am a man of affairs and am but little used to the sly ways of sentiment, but I love you and want you to be my wife. In the city I have gone into society just enough to form a distaste for society women, and I had supposed that I should never entertain the thought of marriage, but you—you have thrilled me, transformed me, compelled me to surrender.

Laura—(*sadly*) I believe you are in earnest, Mr. Radfield, and I shall therefore speak earnestly. It is possible that you do not quite understand your own mind. I am a simple girl, with some pretences to education, it is true, but when brought into comparison with the women of the world I might be found sadly wanting. I am flattered by your offer, I admit, but I cannot marry you. Wait, now. (*Radfield moves impatiently.*) I waited for you and now you must wait for me. I am old-fashioned enough to believe that a woman should love her husband, and I don't love you;

why, our marriage is out of the question. Isn't it, sweetheart? (*Smiling at Gray. Exit.*)

RADFIELD—(*arising and walking up and down the room*) What! it can't be that she is in love with this poor clod. It must not be. With that girl for a wife and with a summer home here, I should be happy. And this sphinx is between us. (*Turning to Gray.*) Well, I'll fix you.

WIDOW—(*without*) Go right on now and wash your face. Go on, this instant!

NAT—(*without*) All time have to be washin' my face. Make Jerry go and wash his face.

Enter Widow and Nat. Widow sighs and takes rocking chair. Nat hangs about her, standing first on one foot and then on the other.

NAT—Want ten cents, now.

WIDOW—Go on away. I'll not give you ten cents.

NAT—Want ten cents, now.

WIDOW—(*making a motion at him*) If you don't go on away, I'll box your jaws.

NAT—Don't give me ten cents I'll thrash the settin' hen off her nest.

WIDOW—Don't you do that, sir; if you do, I'll whip you.

NAT—If you don't give me ten cents, I won't wash my face.

Widow—Well, will you go and wash your face and be a good boy if I give you ten cents?

Nat—Yessum.

Widow—(*giving him money*) There now, dear, go on and be a good boy.

Nat—Won't be good all the time for ten cents. Be good till dinner time. (*Exit N.*)

Jerry—(*without*) Whut you come runnin' er gin me fur, hah? Look whar you gwine, ur de fust thing you know suthin gwine drap an' drap hard, I tell you. (*Enter Jerry.*) Boy come runnin' ergin me like he wuz er calf. Folks all time tryin' run ove' me. Gwine yere suthin drap, too, da is. Er—er—er Miz Morris, I thought I'd come an' ax you ef you kere ef I put on dem britches hangin' in de closet up stairs.

Widow—There are no breeches hanging there.

Jerry—Yassum, da is, caze I hung 'em dar yistidy.

Widow—But what were you doing with them?

Jerry—Why, I wore 'em one ur two times an' hung 'em dar, an' now I 'lowed I ax you ef you kere ef I w'ar 'em ergin. Huh?

Widow—(*almost tearfully*) You trifling rascal, those trousers belonged to my dear husband.

Jerry—(*surprised*) Did da? Wall, I want to tell you dat he wuz er pusson dat knowed whut britches wuz. I yered folks say dat he wuz er mighty smart man, an' da say, too, dat you an' him wuz monstus well suited to one nuder, an' I thought ez he wan't gwine need dem britches ergin, you mout gib 'em ter me. Huh?

WIDOW—Well, yes, you may have them.

JERRY—Thank you, ma'am. Huh! gwine cut a swath 'mung dem ladies now, I tell you. (*Turning to go.*)

RADFIELD—Madam, why don't you make that fellow earn those trousers?

JERRY—Dar's dat white pusson er firin' off dat mouth o' hizen. Ever' time I comes near him he has ter 'sult me. Come er talkin' 'bout er moon in er pictur er keepin' er man er wake. Whut kin yer spect frum er pusson like dat? An' say, pusson, lemme tell you dat you gwine keep on foolin' wid me tell you yere suthin' drap, an' w'en you look roun' ter see whut it is, you'll find yo'self lyin' dar. Huh? (*Exit.*)

RADFIELD—(*to widow*) Why don't you drive that brute off the place?

WIDOW—Why, didn't I tell you that he saved Nat's life? I just couldn't think of driving him away now, and besides he is so much help to me.

(*Gray gets up, walks about the room, looking at the pictures.*)

RADFIELD—I might remember my obligation to him but at the same time I certainly should protect myself against his insolence.

Widow—Oh, he is never insolent to me; indeed, he does everything I tell him to do. (*Gray approaches the door, stands there a moment and exit.*) Poor man, I do pity him.

Radfield—Oh, he's all right. In fact, I think he is to be envied.

Widow—What, a deaf and dumb man to be envied. I don't see how you can make that out.

Radfield—It may be clearer to you when I tell you that your daughter Laura is in love with him.

Widow—(*greatly surprised*) Why, how can you say such a thing, Mr. Radfield?

Radfield—Easily enough. Truth may be pretty scarce, but sometimes it is on hand and then to tell it is not a difficult matter. I know that she is in love with him. I heard her say as much.

Widow—It was only a joke. Laura is too sensible a girl to throw herself away.

Radfield—I wonder then that she is not sensible enough to see something that is to her advantage. I have asked her to be my wife and she has refused.

Widow—(*thoughtfully*) Perhaps she—

Radfield—There is no perhaps about it. She has simply refused to marry me. I hope, madam, that you have no objections to me?

Widow—(*brightening*) I object to you? Surely

not, Mr. Radfield, for never since my poor husband's death have I seen a man—

RADFIELD—I mean of course that I hope you have no objections to me for a son-in-law.

WIDOW—(*sobering*) Yes, I know what you mean. I am surely bright enough to tell what a person means. I don't boast of being very smart but I know enough for that. I hope you don't think—

RADFIELD—Of course not, madam.

WIDOW—Well I'm very glad you don't. Let me see. Well, I don't know that I object to you as a son-in-law, but—there's Harriet.

Enter HARRIET.

HARRIET—Mother, your preserves are boiling over.

WIDOW—(*springs to her feet*) Gracious, why didn't you tell me?

HARRIET—I did.

WIDOW—(*passing quickly through the door*) Jerry, you good-for-nothing thing why did you let them preserves boil over?

JERRY—(*far without*) Doan come talkin' ter me w'en I dun burnt my finger in 'em; soused my finger in dar ter see ef da wuz hot an da wuz.

HARRIET—(*seating herself on the sofa*) Pardon me, but did I hear you tell mother that Laura had refused to be your wife?

Radfield—Yes.

Harriet—Little fool, she never did have any sense. But never mind, she's got to marry you.

Radfield—I am thankful that you champion my cause. I (*Bowles, the detective, appears at the door.*) Come in. Miss Morris will you pardon us for a few minutes. I have some very important business with this man. But wait, you needn't go. What was I thinking about? I can go out with him.

Harriet—(*on her feet*) Oh, no, I was going any way. (*Exit H.*)

Radfield—(*to Bowles*) Sit down.

Bowles—(*continuing to stand*) No, thank you, haven't time. Just stepped in to tell you that I'm going back to town. I don't think there's anything in the case—your suspicions of dummy are not well enough founded.

Radfield—(*rises*) Don't be a fool, man.

Bowles—I have decided not to be and that's the reason I'm going back to town. I know more about this business than you do; I have made a number of mistakes in my time and have decided to profit by them. Good day. (*Turns to go.*)

Radfield—Wait a moment.

Bowles—No use to wait. You have advised me not to be a fool and I have taken your advice. (*Exit B.*)

RADFIELD—Insolent puppy. Those detectives don't know enough to—there you are, eh?

Enter Gray. Walks about the room, paying no attention to Radfield.

RADFIELD—I'm going to get rid of you some way, you blockhead. I believe if you were out of the way everything would be well. And I want you to understand that I'm going to marry that girl. (*Gray stands with his back toward him, looking toward mirror.*) I could brain you and no one would ever be the wiser. (*Looks about.*) I could hit you back of the neck and tell them that you had fallen in a fit. Yes, tell them that you struck your head against the rocker of this chair. (*Moves chair.*) I'm not going to be foiled by you. (*Seizes poker. Gray wheels about with a pistol in one hand and with other hand points at mirror.*)

JERRY—(*poking his head through the door*) Yas, sah, yas sah; de moon in de pictur.

Curtain.

Act III.

TWO DAYS LATER.

SCENE—*Same. Curtain rises, Radfield and Laura discovered in the sitting-room, Laura in rocking chair with book, facing Radfield, who stands with one hand resting on center table.*

Laura—*(looking up from book)* Why did you tell mama that you had asked me to marry you?

Radfield—Perhaps I wanted her to intercede for me.

Laura—As if that would do any good.

Radfield—I didn't know but it might.

Laura—If I were a man I wouldn't marry a girl that had to be begged.

Radfield—*(with a mirthless laugh)* I suppose that is the right view to take of it, but when a man is in love all sensible views are obscured.

Laura—Can you be so much in love as that? I thought that your fancy for me was merely an idle whim.

Radfield—Whims belong to women, men are moved by ideas.

Laura—*(with surprise)* Oh! and is that the reason that some of them move so seldom and so slowly?

Radfield—*(seriously)* Miss Laura, a man may joke while a surgeon is cutting off his arm, but levity does not come from a wounded heart. If a man jokes when his heart aches he is either a fool or a hypocrite.

Laura—You will please pardon me, but I don't think that you love me very much. It is a sort of summer love and will pass away when the frost falls.

Jerry—*(without)* Wonder whar I lef dat ar pipe. Neber seed de like. Man kain't put his pipe down—

(*Enters and looks at Radfield.*) Skuze me, sah, but did you pick up my pipe?

RADFIELD—(*turning contemptuously upon him*) What! Look here; you'll go too far with me the first thing you know. Remember that I am under no obligations to you. You haven't saved me from drowning.

JERRY—(*looking at him with a squint in his eye*) Yas, sah, an' you went too fur wid me de minit you come up ter whar I wuz. How did I know but you mout hab picked up my pipe?

RADFIELD—(*severely*) Get out, you impudent rascal!

JERRY—Dat's zactly whar I wuz gwine, sah. (*Moves to the door, looks back.*) One deze days you gwine yere suthin drap. Mind whut I tells you, an' it gwine drap hard, too. (*Exit J.*)

RADFELD—(*to Laura*) Your mother will never make a success at keeping boarders. By the way, how long is that dummy going to stay?

LAURA—(*looking down at her book*) Mr. Gray will go when he is ready to start, I suppose.

RADFIELD—(*taking a seat*) I shouldn't wonder. By the way, did your mother tell you anything else beside the fact that I had asked you to marry me?

LAURA—(*without looking up*) I don't remember.

RADFIELD—Didn't she tell you that I said that you were in love with Gray?

Laura—(*without taking her eyes from the book*) Isn't he handsome?

Radfield—And his mind is as deaf as his ears.

Laura—And he is so much of a gentleman.

Enter Widow.

Widow—Do I intrude?

Laura—(*looking up*) No, mama, we are so glad you came.

Widow—(*seating herself on the sofa*) I was afraid that you were talking about something that you didn't want me to hear.

Laura—(*laughing*) But a girl ought not to talk about anything that she doesn't want her mother to hear.

Radfield—(*to the widow*) There is thoughtfulness for you.

Widow—Oh, Laura is all the time thoughtful. And all my children are obedient. (*Nat enters and stretches himself upon the floor.*) Get up, son. Don't lie there, you might take cold. Did you hear me? Get up from there and go and wash your face.

Nat—(*turning over*) All time have to wash my face. Why don't you make Jerry wash his face?

Widow—You've got nothing to do with Jerry. Get up, and after awhile I'll give you some preserves.

Nat—Want 'em now.

Widow—Wait until I go out.

Nat—Give 'em to me now or I won't get up.

Widow—All right, sir, I won't let you go to mill with Jerry to-morrow.

Nat—(*brightening*) If I get up will you?

Widow—Yes, if you'll get up and be good.

(*Nat goes to the sofa and lies down with his head in widow's lap.*)

Radfield—(*arising*) Well, I am going out to row. Won't you come along, Miss Laura?

Laura—(*without looking at him*) No, I thank you, I'm tired.

Widow—(*persuasively, to Laura*) Oh, go on with him.

Nat—Mebby if you give her some preserves she will.

Laura—I don't care to go, mama.

Widow—Why, you go with Mr. Gray, and he can't even ask you.

Laura—And probably that's the reason I go.

Radfield—(*to Laura*) Well, will you go this afternoon?

Laura—I'll see about it.

Radfield—That's as good as a promise, I suppose. (*Exit Radfield.*)

Widow—(*to Laura*) Why didn't you go with him?

Laura—Oh, I just couldn't! I don't like him at all, mama.

WIDOW—I wish you wouldn't be so foolish. (*Rises*) You can see how fond he is of you. (*Nat tumbles on the floor.*) Get up, son, and come on. Come, and I'll give you the preserves.

NAT—(*getting up*) And you've got to let me go with Jerry, too, now.

LAURA—(*to widow*) Oh, yes, I can see how fond he is of me, but I can't see how fond I am of him.

WIDOW—(*leading boy toward door*) It does seem to me that a girl ought to look after her own interest ; and times are so hard too. (*Exit widow and boy.*)

LAURA—I wonder if they think I could marry that man. I hate him. (*Gray appears at door.*) Come in sweetheart. (*Gray nods to her and seats himself on sofa.*) Sweetheart, they are trying to take me away from you but they can't. I wonder if he has an idea of what I am talking about?

Enter JERRY.

JERRY—I know I lef dat pipe summers. Huh, (*looking at Gray*) yere's dat pusson dat kain't talk. But I want to tell you what, (*looking at Laura*) he's er fine pusson. Come a givin' me a quarter jest de same ez ef he could make a speech. I doan blebe it make so much diffunce whuther er man kin talk ur not. I know folks dat has been er talkin' all dar lives an' neber has 'mounted ter nuthin' yit. Yas, I does.

(*Feels in his pockets. Draws out a pipe.*) Why, yere dat triflin' pipe. Huh, whut's gittin' de matter wid me? But I wanter tell you right now dat it wuz er powerful good thing dat it wan't tuck by dat pusson dat called me er rascal. Mind whut I tell you, he gwine yer suthin drap (*Exit J.*)

LAURA—(*looking at Gray*) That's the funniest negro you ever saw, sweetheart; and one of these times if I learn to talk on my fingers, I may tell you about the funny things he does. Oh, I'm so sorry for you. A bird flew to the top of the house this morning and sat there and sang ever so long, and you didn't hear his song. I thought of you at the time. How many people hear the songs of birds and are too dull to be thrilled. But you'd be thrilled if you could hear, wouldn't you sweetheart?

Enter HARRIET.

HARRIET—What are you doing here, Laura?

LAURA—Oh, just talking to my sweetheart.

HARRIET—(*frowning at her and taking a chair*) You ought to be ashamed of yourself.

LAURA—(*innocently*) Why, just because I talk to my sweetheart? Oh, sister, I am astonished at you. Why, if you had a sweetheart, wouldn't you talk to him? You have had sweethearts, and didn't you talk to them?

HARRIET—(*moving angrily in her chair*) I wish you did have some little sense, Laura.

LAURA—How little?

HARRIET—(*flouncing*) Oh, don't talk to me!

LAURA—Well, then, I must talk to my sweetheart.

HARRIET—Silliest goose I ever saw. Why didn't you go boat riding with Mr. Radfield?

LAURA—Oh, because I was tired.

HARRIET—No, you were not anything of the sort, and you know it.

LAURA—Yes, if I wasn't I know it.

HARRIET—Goose! (*After a pause*) Mr. Radfield is going home to-morrow.

LAURA—Oh, is he going to put it off so long as that?

HARRIET—You ought to be ashamed of yourself. First thing you know you'll have all the neighbors saying that you are in love with a deaf and dumb man.

LAURA—Yes? I wonder when they are going to begin. We might get up a sort of a picnic for the occasion. Oh, I'll tell Jerry to get some Chinese lanterns when he goes to the village.

Enter widow with Nat tagging after her.

WIDOW—(*taking a seat and holding Nat on her lap*) I'll be glad when night comes, I'm so tired.

HARRIET—You wouldn't have to work so hard if Laura had any sense,

LAURA—Isn't that unfortunate! Do you know what I am going to do? I'm going to get my books and study as hard as I can. Then, you see, I'll soon have more sense.

HARRIET—(*flouncing*) Oh, don't talk to me.

LAURA—All right, I'll talk to my sweetheart.

HARRIET—(*to widow*) Mother, I'd make her quit that foolishness.

WIDOW—(*to Laura*) You must stop it, dear.

LAURA—Why, what harm is there in it? He can't hear me?

WIDOW—I know, but other people can.

LAURA—Oh, well, what if they do? they must know that I am simply joking.

WIDOW—But it is better not to carry on that way. Some people can't understand a joke. Nat, (*shaking him*) go over there and sit down. You wear me out.

NAT—What will you give me?

WIDOW—Oh, anything! Go over there and sit down on the sofa.

NAT—By him? I'm afraid I'd catch it.

HARRIET—(*to Nat*) Catch what, simpleton?

NAT—That—that not knowin' how to talk.

HARRIET—And it would be a good thing for you.

Enter RADFIELD.

HARRIET—(*rising*) Have this seat, Mr. Radfield.

RADFIELD—No, I thank you, I don't care to sit down. I have come merely to tell you good bye.

HARRIET—Oh, you don't mean it!

RADFIELD—Yes, I must get back to town.

Gray gets up and goes out.

WIDOW—We are so sorry to lose you.

RADFIELD—I wish you could speak for every one when you say that. (*Looks at Laura.*)

HARRIET—Oh, she can, I'm sure. But will you not come back soon?

RADFIELD—I may, but I can't tell how soon. I have had—I was going to say a pleasant time, but perhaps I should say an impressive time.

Enter Gray. Stands with his back to the fireplace, facing the rest of the company.

HARRIET—Is Mr. Gray going with you?

RADFIELD—(*with an air of apology*) I know nothing of the intentions of our unfortunate friend. (*Looks at Laura.*)

LAURA—Yes, it is unfortunate not to hear some things, and still, as you once said to sister, it is fortunate not to hear other things.

RADFIELD—Yes, I believe I said something like that. I am pleased to know that you even remember——

LAURA—(*interrupting him*) Oh, I never forget anything.

Radfield—That gives me a hope that you may not forget me.

Laura—(*as though she did not hear him*) Yes, I remember the good and the bad alike, I suppose.

Widow—You will want Jerry to take you to the station, won't you?

Radfield—I should prefer some one else. (*Looks at Laura.*) Can't you drive me out?

Laura—I'm afraid of the horse.

Harriet—I will drive you, Mr. Radfield.

Radfield—(*bowing*) I thank you, but surely I do not wish to put you to that trouble.

Harriet—No trouble, but a pleasure.

Harriet arises and Radfield steps toward the door. Gray with a quick movement reaches the door first, turns and confronts him.

Gray—Stop! Stand where you are! (*Every one starts up in astonishment.*) Ladies, I have been forced to deceive you. My name is not Gray. I am George Miller, a reporter for a Chicago newspaper, and I have been set on track of this man, to fasten the proof of a robbery upon him. He is the man who has robbed the express office, his own company. Don't you move! (*To Radfield.*) Outside are two deputy sheriffs waiting for you. Oh, I've got the absolute proof on you.

Laura—(*hiding her face*) And oh! he's got the absolute proof on me, too!

Gray—Yes, I have, and that proof is that you are the sweetest and most charming woman in the world. (*Holds out his hands; she slowly approaches him and he takes her hands.*)

Jerry—(*poking his head in at the door*) Whut I dun tole you 'bout, dat suthin' gwine drap? Ur moon in er picture, er—haw! haw!

Curtain.

HIS SIXTEEN-EIGHTY-NINE.

CHAPTER I.

OFF Dearborn street in Chicago, there is an old book—"joint,"—that has long been known to people who find a musty delight in old style type and musty bindings. It is a cellar, approached by a dark and narrow stairway, and many a man, attracted thither by stories that were told of the place, have turned back in disgust when half way down the stairs. The old cellar was of itself as musty as a rare first edition, and was but dimly lighted, but the eager eyes of a true bibliomaniac soon discovered the beauties of this, the wayward hiding place of weary learning, abashed fancies and murdered ambitions. The walls were covered with books, and the corners were stacked and jammed with old political pamphlets. What records of the law's injustice; what demands for reformations that never came!

This place, known as the "Book-worm's Joint," was kept by an old man named Dorsey. He was once the proprietor of an old book stall in London. Why he left the world's relic house of literature and settled in Chicago is not known, nor does it materially affect this recital. I don't know how the old man would have appeared in the sunlight, for I never saw him there, but amid the shadows of his "joint," he was most impressive. His hair was long and white; his flowing gray beard seemed to be kept as a sort of religion. He was tall, and bent and feeble. His eyes were of a mildewed brown, in color, and were so weak that he could scarcely read a newspaper—to-day's "pert" infringement on the learning of yore—but with the swift glance of intuition he could discern the faded title of an ancient tome. Visitors of a certain class were welcome, but purchasers seemed to alarm him. He was compelled to sell books, for he had no other source of income, but it gave him pain to part with a volume, and once, when the necessity of meeting his rent had forced him to sell the political pamphlets of DeFoe, he fell upon his miserable bed and moaned as if his heart would break. He was a book miser. The disastrous year to the commercial world was a year of comparative prosperity to old Dorsey, for then he was not so much assailed by customers. As time passed he grew worse and hugged his books in an embrace of despair.

One afternoon a collector called and presented him a bill.

"What is it for?" the old man asked, tremblingly adjusting his glasses.

"December rent."

"But I paid it the other day, didn't I?"

"No, you paid for November about a month ago."

"It seems to me, young man, that you were here the other day and that I paid you for December."

"I can't help how it seems to you. I know my business, I reckon."

"Well, how much is the amount?"

"You ought to know. You've paid it often enough."

"Ah, I grant you that," he replied, scanning the bill. "What!" he suddenly exclaimed, "forty dollars! You have raised on me."

"No, we haven't. It's been forty dollars for the last four years."

"But I don't think I ought to pay so much, young man."

"Well, then, get out. A fellow wants to start a Turkish bath in here, anyway."

"Oh, no, no; I can't do that. I have been here so long that I am attached to the place."

"Well, then, pay your rent."

"I will, but I can't do it to-day. Come around some other time."

"I will come to-morrow, and if you don't pay then

you may know what to expect. It's growing harder and harder to get money out of you, and we're getting tired of it. See?"

The collector went out, and Dorsey, turning to a man who had just entered, asked: "Can I do anything for you, sir?"

"Well, I don't know," the man answered, slowly turning about the room. "Thought I'd drop in and look around. Have you a catalogue?"

"No, sir."

"Ought to issue one every once in a while."

"That would be unnecessary, sir, as I don't add to my stock."

"Humph, you don't do a very thriving business."

"No. To tell the truth I don't care to do any business. I did at first, though. I used to purchase largely and get out a catalogue every three months but now I—the truth is, I have only the books that I am attached to and don't want to part with them."

"Ha! rather a strange case. But you must have made considerable money while you were actively in the business."

"Yes, I made some, but lost it. Do you remember fifteen years ago when the steamship 'McAlpin' was lost?"

"Yes, believe I do."

"I had twenty-five thousand dollars worth of books

on board, and their loss discouraged me so that I have never taken much of an interest in business since."

"I see; and the keeping of this place is now a sort of sentiment with you."

"Well, I suppose you might term it a sentiment. I have lived in this cellar so long that I could not find contentment elsewhere. I should be like the prisoner who begged to be re-admitted into his cell; and these books are my family. I part with one sometimes—and so does a man bury his children sometimes."

"Yes, that's true."

The visitor began to browse about, with the slow motion of carelessness, but with an eye of cool and careful search.

"What have we here?"

"One of the earliest English edititions of Plutarch," the old man answered with strange excitement, and then quickly reached out to take the volume.

"Let me look at it," said the visitor, turning about.

"Oh, I don't think you will like it, sir. It hasn't been very well cared for, and I fancy that the binding wasn't very good in the first place. Indeed, sir," he added, becoming more eager to take the book, "I don't believe that it is so old as its date would imply. 1689 —I don't really believe it is so old as that. I haven't looked into the matter very closely, not being much interested, you know, but I don't believe there was an English translation of Plutarch so far back as that."

"The deuce there wasn't," the visitor replied; "how did Shakespeare manage to follow Plutarch's Julius Cæsar so closely?"

"Well, but Shakespeare may have been a better scholar than Ben. Jonson thought he was. Indeed, sir, great men have begun to believe that Bacon wrote the plays,—at least the classic ones."

"Rats!" said the visitor. "How many volumes are there of this?"

"Eight, and you see what unwieldly things they are."

"What will you take for the set?"

"Really, sir, I think I have an edition that will suit you much better."

"Don't want any other edition; want this. What will you take for it?"

"I don't want to sell it," he said, taking the volume from the visitor.

"It isn't so rare, old man, that it is priceless. I will give you seventy-five dollars."

"The price is satisfactory enough, but I don't care to sell."

"But don't you need money? Didn't I hear a man say just now that unless you pay him forty dollars to-morrow, steps will be taken to turn you into the street?"

"Yes, that's a fact; yes."

"Then, why are you so foolish?"

"My dear sir, I wouldn't order a man out of my house for the world, but won't you please go away? I am sick and must lie down."

"Yes, I will go away, but I will come back to-morrow."

The visitor went out and the old man, gathering up his precious volumes, tenderly placed them on his bed, and then laid down beside them. Hours passed and still he continued to lie there. Once some one came in, and coughed to attract his attention, but he did not look up. He dozed off into a troubled dream, and was awakened by voices in the "joint." He got up, and, after rubbing his dim old eyes, recognized two acquaintances.

"Hello, Dorsey."

"Good evening, gentlemen."

"You may well say evening if you wish to refer to the lateness of the hour."

"What time is it?"

"After twelve."

"I had no idea it was so late," the old man said, getting up and coming forward.

"You were not awake to hear the news."

"What news?"

"A bank just up the street was robbed of fifteen

thousand dollars this evening. But I don't suppose it concerns you much?"

"Well, I can't say that I'm shocked, still the news is interesting. If somebody had to be robbed I don't know of an institution that is more able to lose money than a bank. It is much better, too, than if an old book store had been robbed. Won't you come back and sit down?"

"No, just thought we'd drop in a moment and look round. Good night."

CHAPTER II.

The first thing Dorsey thought of the next morning, was that he had to pay his rent that day. But he had strong hopes that he might make enough of what he termed comparatively indifferent sales to raise forty dollars; yet the morning wore away and no one came in. Just at noon the collector entered the place.

"Well, have you got forty dollars for me?"

"I am sorry to say that I haven't. I expected some money this morning but it didn't come. But I am sure it will be here by to-morrow. Anything I can do for you, sir?" he asked, turning to a man who had just entered, and then he drew back for he recognized the man who had offered seventy-five dollars for Plutarch.

"Yes," the man answered, "you can let me have those books."

"But I told you——"

"Never mind what you told me. Here are seventy-five dollars, nearly enough to pay two months rent. Come, now, don't be foolish. You'll soon forget the attachment you had for them. You don't want to be set out in the street. Here, give the man his rent."

"But he can't put me out under a month and by that time I'll have the money."

"Well, but what's the use of hanging fire over a thing that must be done?"

A long discussion followed. The would-be purchaser was persuasive and logical; the old man finally yielded in a sort of dreamy way. The persistent customer marched off with his books and the collector went away with his rent.

Old Dorsey's eyes were more than ever a mildewed brown, and his flowing beard, which had seemed to be kept as a sort of religion, was tangled as no creed ought to be. Sometimes he would mumble as if talking apologetically to some one, and then he would break out as if in a fierce argument. Late one night he was pacing up and down the room when an odd and cautious-looking man came down the narrow stairway.

"Who are you?" the old man demanded, and then

added, when the visitor halted: "I have paid the rent."

"Glad of it," the visitor answered.

"Well, but why do you come back here? Is it possible that another month has passed?"

"I don't know what you are talking about."

"Didn't you come around here this morning and collect forty dollars from me?"

"I never saw you before."

"Is that so?" and, then, after a few moments' silence, during which he rubbed his dim, old eyes, he added: "Well, what do you want here now?"

"Just thought I'd drop in and warm myself. Didn't reckon you'd care."

"Of course I don't, but let me see if you are a first edition."

The fellow laughed and said: "I reckon I am. That is, my father and mother always said I was the oldest of five children."

"What's your date?"

"1850, I understand."

"And not 1689?"

"Hah, you must think I'm just out of the ark."

"Hardly so old as that, but when were you first translated? You know it has been held by certain scholars, or I may say alleged scholars, that a versatile monk put you into crude English before the art of printing was invented. How about that—but, pray pardon me, I thought for a moment you were 'Plutarch's Lives.'"

"Well, now, I ain't and never was anybody's life but my own."

The old man rubbed his brow and said: "It was a long time before I could believe in the occult, but I am becoming a full-fledged mystic. It is something that all sensible men must come to. But mysticism is too grand to be grasped at once. It is the key to all wisdom; and there can be no sorrow when all men are just and wise, for justice relieves the wants of the body and wisdom will provide against grief."

"Have you got anything to eat handy?" the visitor asked, glancing about.

"I wish I had Greek wine and pomegranates," the old man answered, "but I haven't. You are welcome, though, to what I have. Here is a beefsteak pie," he added, taking a plate from a shelf and handing it to the visitor. "You see I still keep my English appetite."

"Thanks."

The fellow seized the pie and began eagerly to devour it. The old man stood watching him. The fellow's eyes bulged out. "Got any water?" he asked, almost choked. The old man handed him a leaking dipper of water. "I am old fashioned even in my drinking," he said. The old fellow walked back to his bed, turned despairingly toward the door, confusedly put out his hands before him, and then, wheeling about and facing his guest, who was swallowing the last morsel of the meat pie, said in tremulous tones:

"I thank heaven that you have returned."

"Good enough, but as I never was here before I don't see how I could have returned."

"But didn't a brisk and heartless business man give me seventy-five dollars for you?"

"If he gave you any money for me I wish you would let me have it."

"Oh my 1689!" cried the old man, attempting to fling his arms about the fellow, "Oh, my Plutarch, I will never part with you again."

"What kind of a joint have I struck?"

"You have come home and you will never leave me again."

"Much obliged to you for your kindness but I've got my own affairs to look after. It's gettin' along toward mornin' and I reckon I'd better go."

"You can not go, my Plutarch. Ah, what binding, what print. There are none like you these days. Tell me, did the disturbed elements foretell Cæsar's death? In the dreams of an anxious mind did the fountain spurt blood?"

"I give it up."

"But did Alexander ride the fiery horse that Philip

was unable to master? I know that you are a romancer, and that you have talked much for the mere pleasure of listening to your own musical words, but you can tell an old worshipper many truths that you withheld, even from Montaigne."

"Cap, your water is too deep for me. Let me get out." The old man was standing between his guest and the door.

"No, you are not going to leave me."

"I've got to go. Get out of the way," he said, attempting to pass the old man. "I don't want to stay down here with a crazy man. Let me by, I say. Turn me loose. I'll choke the life out of you. Get away."

The old man fell on the floor, and desperately clung to the fellow's knees.

"Turn me loose, you old fool, or I'll tramp the life out of you."

The old man uttered a loud and despairing cry. Footsteps on the stairway—police. They seized the fellow; they knew him—had been searching for him. He was the bank robber.

The old man, still grieving over his loss, is in the asylum at Kankakee.

BIG HEP AND LITTLE LADY.

WHEN the superintendent of a railway, that had just been built through Allen county, Kentucky, published an announcement that he would buy all the cord-wood that might be ricked up at certain places along his road, the news flew as a carrier pigeon, conveying the words of promised deliverance from the cutthroat mortgage of the crossroads merchant. The country was exceedingly poor. The hillside fields were trenched with gullies, and the gushing rain-tide had washed away so much of the soil that many a patch of land, which at its best was capable of producing only nubbins, would not now have sprouted a black-eyed pea. Along the creeks there was strips of comparatively fertile land, but they were subject to overflow and were not, even after the kindliest season, productive of sufficient grain to keep their owners out of debt. It was early spring when the superintendent's publication was received, and instantly there was an unhitching of old plow horses, and a throwing of old bull-tongue plows into the fence corners.

It was like a call to arms in a patriotic community;

it seemed to be the movement of a single impulse. Every able-bodied man shouldered his axe and turned toward the "big woods," a great and rugged forest which was yet the common property of mankind. Cabins were built, and patches here and there in the woods soon bore the aspect of a mining camp.

Hep Brooks was one of the first men to build a cabin. He was known as Big Hep; and he was a giant. He was splendidly proportioned, and Bradford Wellbanks, an old circuit-rider who lost his life recently while attempting to save a worthless fellow from drowning, often pleasantly remarked that he would bet his saddle-bags that Big Hep could outrun a buck and kill him with his fist after he caught him. Hep was about twenty-five years old, and although he was a rather good-looking fellow, had never spent much time in the society of women. It was soon remarked that he was adorning his cabin with many an extra touch, and one evening a neighbor said to him that he must be thinking of making some woman happy.

"I am," he answered.

"That's right, for you're gittin' old enough. This is a mighty fine place for women up here in the hills and they can help a right smart chance when we begin to haul the wood down to the road. When air you goin' to git married?"

"You air too hard for me now," said Hep.

"Why, I thought you 'lowed you was goin' to make some woman happy."

"So I did, but makin' a woman happy don't always mean marryin'. This cabin "—pointing with pride to the hut—" is for my mother."

"Oh, I didn't know that. By the way I don't believe I ever seed her."

"No, I reckon not. She is livin' over in Barren county with my brother Jim an' never has been out to Allen. You know I ain't been livin' here but about two years; come out here to see if I couldn't git a place for her, but it 'peared like the harder I worked the wus times got, and I was jest about to give up and go somewhar else when this wood business come up. It won't take me long now to knock out a few dollars."

"I reckon not, but have you made any arrangements about havin' yo' wood hauled down to the road?"

"That was about the only thing that stood in my way, not havin' airy hoss, but I have agreed to pay Sim Joyner so much to haul it out and rick it up for me. I've got to strike out early in the mornin' atter mother."

"I reckon you'll have some little trouble in hirin' a hoss to go that fur."

"Yes, a good deal. The truth is I kain't git a hoss at all, but I'll fetch her all right enough."

Hep set out early the next morning while his neighbors were eating breakfast. He disappeared down the valley, singing his one tuneless song:

> "Oh, the old raccoon was chased from his hole,
> And he couldn't git back for to save his soul.
> He tried it late and he tried it soon,
> But he couldn't git back, that old raccoon."

Four days passed before they heard that tuneless song again, and then they heard it coming up out of the valley.

"I don't see his mother with him," a man remarked, shading his eyes with his hand. "Mebby the old lady couldn't walk so fur. He's got a pretty big bundle of something on his back."

They stood speculating until Hep came up, and then they saw a woman's head protruding from a roll of blanket which the giant carried on his back. Every one uttered an exclamation of surprise when Hep placed his mother in a hickory sapling chair which he had made for her, and which he requested some one to bring from the cabin.

"Now you sit right here, Little Lady, till I git you suthin' to eat," said the giant. "You see," he pleasantly added, turning to his neighbors, "that thar's a good deal of diffunce in our size. I weigh over two hundred and Little Lady don't weigh but ninety."

"And is she r'a'ly yo' mother?" some one asked.

"Indeed I am," the little, old woman spoke up. "And if you had seed Hep onct long time ago you wouldn'ter thought he would be much when he growd up. But bless us all, jest look at him now."

How sweet and pleased her old face was. She had that peculiar countenance which seems to come as an illumined beauty to old age—a face through which one catches glimpses of a patient and loving soul. She looked like a mere doll, and was as easily amused as a child. Big Hep brought his axe and showed it to her, and when he explained that he had experienced some trouble in finding one large enough for him, she seized the arms of the chair and laughed.

CHAPTER II.

Hep's house became a favorite resort, and at evening the neighbors would gather there and sing religious songs. They knew no worldly airs, and to them music was the handmaiden of the gospel. The leader of the musical exercises was a girl named Lutie Moore. She was the daughter of a man who owned several teams, and was, therefore, high in the social grade. She had the appearance of a flirt, and it was known that she had smiled upon Rob Turner, as hard a working young fellow as ever lived, and then refused to marry him, although he begged her piteously and although he was a hard-working boy. It was soon discovered that Big Hep was smitten with her, and one Sunday when he hired one of her father's horses and took her to church, at least ten miles distant, the gossips knew that a marriage or a refusal would be the result. Old Miss Beverly, the chief of gossips, called on Hep's mother that Sunday, and the impulse to gossip was so strong within her that she disregarded her usual skirmishing and went at once into the engagement.

"I reckon you know that Hep's gone with Lute Moore to-day."

"Yes," the little, old woman answered, "but I reckon he'll come back."

"Oh, of course, but haven't you been thinkin' that he mout want to marry her?"

"The only thing I've thought about it is that she would have to search a mighty long time before she could do better."

"I understand that, too, but ain't you afeered she won't have him, and that it will pretty nigh break his heart?"

"He has a mighty big heart, Miss Beverly."

"That's true enough, but big hearts air ginerally the

easiest to break. Look at Rob Turner, fur instance. Thar ain't nobody got no bigger heart than he has, and thar ain't a harder workin' boy in all this country, and now look at him. He mopes about like he don't kere whuther the price of wood keeps up or not. If I had a son—and I reckon it's a blessin' that I ain't—I would hate to see him makin' a set at a girl like Lute Moore. I would jest give him a piece of sensible advice. I would tell him to be keerful of women that thinks themselves good lookin' an' take some good, honest person that thinks more of other folks than she does of herself. I would tell him to find some good girl, makes no difference if she was a little older than him, and marry her. I have been mightily interested in Hep ever sense I fust seed him, and I do so much want him to git a good wife whenever he do marry."

"Little Lady," with all her smallness physically, and beauty born of a sweet and patient soul, was a woman, and while Miss Beverly was talking this little mother mused: "I see what you air drivin' at, Missie, but you might as well hush, for Hep will never marry such a lookin' busy-body as you air. Why, thar wouldn't be no livin' in the house with you."

"Well, I must go," said Miss Beverly, rising. "I thought I would merely drop over and see you awhile.

I wish—but never mind—" She was now standing in the door, twisting the strings of her gingham sunbonnet.

"What were you goin' to wish?"

"Oh, nuthin', only I thought that if you cared to speak of it, you might tell Hep that we air all might'ly interested in him. I don't think I ever seen a young man that I ever was more interested in than I am in him. Good mornin'."

When Hep returned from church, late that evening, his mother looked at him closely, as if she were searching for evidences of unrequited love; and when he had sat down to the table upon which his dinner had been spread, she noticed that he did not eat with his usual relish.

"What's the matter, Hep?"

"Oh, nuthin'," he answered, looking up surprised. "What makes you think thar's anything the matter?"

"I didn't think you eat like you had much appetite, and thar is the dandelion greens, too."

"I won't try to fool you, Little Lady," he said, smiling. "I will jest tell you exactly what is the matter. I love Lutie Moore."

"And do she love you, my son?"

"That's what I kain't find out."

"Have you said anything to her about it?"

"Not yet. I have been tryin' to all day, but somehow I couldn't. I'd keep on lookin' ahead and think that when I got thar I would say somethin', but I kep' puttin' it off, an' puttin' it off, till here I am an' nuthin' ain't been said yit."

"Do you want me to go over and talk to her?"

"Gracious, no!" he exclaimed. "She would think that I ain't got sense enough to talk fur myself, and that would settle it right then and thar. The next time the folks come over here to sing I will walk home with her and say somethin' or bust a hame-string, as pap uster say."

The singing party met that very night, and Hep walked home with Lutie Moore. He struggled with himself as they walked along, and not until they had almost arrived at Moore's cabin could he summon up sufficient courage. Finally, in a sort of desperate burst, he exclaimed:

"Stop right here whar you air and let me say suthin'." She stopped and turned her face toward him. The moon was shining.

"Miss Lutie," said he, "I want to tell you somethin' that I have tried mighty hard to say. I never was much of a hand to go among women, for the reason that I never was much interested in their talk, but it's different with you. It don't make no difference what you say, I am interested in it; and I don't believe you could say a word that wouldn't sorter stir me up. What have you got to say to that?" he added, his desperation giving away to embarrassment.

"I don't know what you mean," she said.

"Wall, I mean jest this here! I love you; and now what have you got to say to that?"

"I say that I am glad of it."

"Air you railly!" he exclaimed, placing his hands on her head. "Air you sho nuff, and air you glad enough to love me?"

"Yes," she said smiling, and the moon that shone full in her face pointed out the smile to him.

He scarcely remembered anything else that night, except that he hastened home and told his mother that he was almost too happy to live.

"Lift me up and kiss me," said the little, old woman.

He got up the next morning singing his one tuneless song. "And you won't forget me after you are married, will you son?" the little woman asked.

He sat down, looked at her a moment, and said: "I don't see what could have put that into yo' little head. I love that girl well enough to die for her, but I couldn't love her well enough to forgit you."

The gossips soon learned of Hep's engagement, and there was great surprise when it was reported that Lutie was "dead in love" with him. "And her father owns so many teams, too," one woman remarked. "Sholy, strange things do happen in this here world."

* * * * * *

The night was beautiful; the wedding was to take place on the following day. Big Hep and Lutie sat on a log. They could hear "Little Lady" singing.

"Hep," said the girl, "we'll be so happy after we air married."

"Yes, the happiest of anybody in the world," he answered.

"And then yo' won't have no trouble in gittin' hosses to haul yo' wood. Say, dear, how long is yo' mother goin' to stay with you?"

"Allus," Hep proudly answered.

"No, that mustn't be. I like her well enough, but I'm afeerd she would make me tired."

He arose, looked down upon her for a moment and then said: "And if that's the case, I reckon I would make you tired, too. I worship you—or did worship you—but the Lord has p'inted out my duty. Good-night."

"But wait, Hep, tell me that we air to be married in the mornin'."

"Good-night," he repeated.

* * * * * *

The neighbors that arose early the next morning,

saw Hep, with a large bundle on his back, going down into the valley, and they heard the words of his tuneless song:

> "Oh, the old raccoon was chased from his hole,
> And he couldn't git back for to save his soul.
> He tried it late and he tried it soon,
> But he couldn't git back, that old raccoon."

AN IVORY SMILE.

CHAPTER I.

The following sketch, written by Col. J. McCloud, of Kentucky, was recently given to me by a son of that well-known gentleman:

I lived in Kentucky and owned a number of slaves. Among them was an enormous man, named Amos. I think he was the strongest human being I ever have seen. Once when I was a boy I went with Amos to a circus. During the performance the ring-master announced that he had a wonderful mule. "I will give this mule to any man who can either ride him or lead him around the ring." Amos arose. I plucked his coat and excitedly asked what he was going to do. I asked this, although I knew well enough what was on his mind.

"Chile," said he, "dar ain't no man, white nur black, dat's gwine bluff me wid er mule;" and before I could by persuasion restrain him, he had stalked into the ring. The mule was a small animal and depended for success upon that quality which so well serves the small man and the politician—trickery. Amos turned to the ring-master and said:

"You means dat I kin hab dis mule ef I kin ride him ur lead him?"

"That is exactly what I mean."

"Ah, hah, an' does you mean dat ef I takes dis yere mule outen de ring I kin hab him?"

"Yes, if you can take him out of the ring he is your property."

Amos seized the mule and I don't know how, but in a moment had him on his back. The frightened animal struggled, but Amos, amid the wildest applause, carried him out of the ring.

"He's mine," Amos shouted as he put down his burden.

"Not so fast, my good fellow," the ring-master cried, quickly following him. "I said you might have him if you could lead him out of the ring."

"An' den you said I could hab him ef I tuck him out?"

"Oh, no," the ring-master answered, taking hold of the bridle. "I said if you could lead him; but now to show that there's nothing mean about me, I will solemnly swear in the presence of these good people, that I will give you the elephant if you take him on your shoulder down to the river and give him a bath."

The audience roared as though the world's greatest

witticism had just been uttered, and Amos, disgusted with the perfidy of showmen, returned to his seat.

I was deeply attached to Amos, who, my father assured me was my individual property; and I used to smile over the absurdity of so small a boy owning so large a man. When I grew up, and when the death of my father gave to me the sad inheritance of all the slaves, I depended on Amos as a sort of general manager. He was so faithful and had so apparent an affection for me, that in gratitude and especially in a Christian prompting, I resolved to set him free. So, one day just before Christmas, I called him as he was crossing the yard.

"Good mawnin', Mars George; how does you feel dis mawnin', sah?"

"First-rate, Amos. In fact, I feel so well that I have decided to give you a great Christmas present."

"Thankee, sah," he replied, removing his hat and bowing low, "an' lemme tell you dat de Lawd ain't gwine furgit you fur dat. Lawd dun said He is mighty in lub wid de cheerful giber, an' ef you ain't one I doan know who is. Look yere, Mars George, whut it gwine be?"

"Never mind, I'll tell you when Christmas morning comes."

"Dat's right an' proper, sah, but somehow I'd like ter hab er little sorter idee. I wanter know how ter shape myself. Man 'pear like he wanter be s'prized, but still he'd ruther know whut he gwine be s'prized erbout. When de dog trees er 'possum er man would like ter be s'prized ez ter whut sort o' varment dar is up dar, still he'd ruther know whuther it's er 'possum ur er coon 'fo' he chops down de tree."

"That's all right, Amos, but you go ahead and cut down the tree and leave it to me to provide against disappointment."

"Wall, ez you nebber has diserp'inted me, I'll do dat. I got up ter go ober in de woods, sah, an' see erbout hawlin' up some back-logs fur Christmas. Doan want none de white folks ter git cold on dat day, I as-sho you. Dar ain't nuthin' dat takes de brightness offen Christmas day like chilly white folks. Good mawnin', Mars George."

He went away, singing the blithe song of a light heart. He was a giant but he was a child.

Before daylight, one morning shortly afterward, while I was yet in bed, a house servant tapped on the door and told me that Amos wanted to see me. "Tell him to come in," I answered. The giant, black in the dark shadows of the dim lamp-light and the early morning, entered the room and stood near my bedside. There was the sudden gleam of an ivory smile, then a low, musical laugh and the warm tones of a "good mawnin', Mars George."

"Well, Amos, what do you want this time of day?"

"Dat's whut I come ter tell you, sah. I woke up 'bout midnight, an' 'fo' de Lawd I couldn't go ter sleep ergin fur 'layin' dar worryin'."

"What about?"

"Wall, sah, jes dis: I wuz wonderin' whut in de worl' you gwine gib me fur dat Christmus present. Now I know you gwine turn ober wid one dem flounces de white folks has, an' say I'se foolish an' ain't got no sense, an' I 'low mebbe you'd be right ef you did say so, but I jest couldn't he'p it, Mars George."

But I did not turn over with one of those flounces that the "white folks" have; I reached out and took his hand. "My poor child," said I, "my poor child ——" and I really could say nothing else. He broke down. The giant was on his knees.

"Oh, you calls me er chile, when it wa'n't but de udder day dat I toted you in my arms, showing you de geese swimmin' in de pond, an' now you is er gre't big man an' calls me chile. Ole Marster's time does fly monstrus fast when de little toddler o' yistidy terday takes you by de han' like he gwine lead you, an' calls you chile. But I wush you would tell me whut dat present gwine be. It doan 'pear like I kin stand it no longer, Mars George." With the tenderness of a mother's touch his hand stroked my hair. "Tell me jest dis time, Mars George, an' I won't ax you no mo'."

"Amos, you have only two more days to wait, and I don't believe that it would be real kindness to tell you now."

"Wall, sah," he said, slowly arising to his feet, "it will hatter go, I reckon. Ain't dar er jug in dat closet, sah? Dat one right dar?"

"Yes, I think so."

"Wall, would you mind ef I wuz ter tilt it up ez er sort o' good mawnin' ter dis new-bo'n day, sah?"

"Help yourself, Amos."

"I thanks you, I does. Ef dar's anythin' dat smooths out de wrinkles o' er diserp'intment, it's one deze fine articles o' licker."

He drew out the jug and tilted a long good morning to the new-born day, and then, slowly wiping his mouth with the back of his hand, declared that he was strengthened against the trials of another season of disappointment.

He did not again speak of the present until early Christmas morning. Then he came and tapped on my bedroom door.

"Mars George, oh, Mars George."

"Is that you, Amos?"

"Yas, sah, an' I come ter 'mind you dat Chris'mas done come."

"I know that, Amos."

"Yas, sah, I 'lowed you did, but I wuz sorter

skeered dat ole Satan mout put suthin' in yo' way ter make you furgit it."

"You haven't known him to put many things in my way to make me forget promises, have you?"

"No, sah, but still you kain't nebber tell what Satan gwine do. De Good Book say he allus pokin' round seekin' whut he kin 'vower."

"Well, I'll be out pretty soon, and give you the present."

"All right, sah, but you ain't gwine turn ober an' go ter sleep ergin, is you?"

"No, I'm getting up now;" and then I heard him mutter: "thank de Lawd fur dat."

There had been so much speculation among the negroes as to what Amos' present was to be, that I was greeted by nearly every man, woman and child on the plantation when I stepped out upon the veranda. I shall never forget that morning. The sun was rising. Far in the west the loitering stars were fading one by one, and above them hung the quartered moon, stripped of her majesty and paled by the brightening glory of the morn. Far down the creek, where the lurking shadows hid under the bending willow boughs, the rushing waters played a deep-toned symphony, and in the woods a tired dog, barked unheeded, where he had "treed" at midnight.

"Amos," I said, stepping forward.

"Yas, Mars George," he answered, bowing.

"I promised you a Christmas present, and in view of my great attachment, you, with reason, supposed that it was to be something to be valued far above the ordinary gift."

"Yas, Mars George."

"Amos, I am going to give you something which many of the world's greatest men have died for, and for which any great man would shed his blood. Amos, I give you freedom."

He did not bound into the air, as I had expected; he wiped his mouth with the back of his hand, and quietly said:

"I 'lowed you gwine gimme dat 'possum dog."

"What! You old rascal," I exclaimed, "would you rather have a dog than your freedom?"

He looked up and thus replied: "Er ole man kin hab comfort wid er 'possum dog, sah, but when freedom comes ter er ole man it makes him feel foolish."

"Amos, you are not so old. I will give you two hundred dollars, and you can go away and be a free man. Although I am deeply attached to you, yet I would not advise you to stay here. Come, and I will give you the money."

CHAPTER II.

YEARS passed, and the war came. I went as a captain into the Confederate army. I shall say but little of my military career, for there is but a small part of it that concerns this narration. While on a raid in Kentucky I was captured. A number of depredations had been committed upon Union men, and I was charged with these wanton outrages. I was innocent, but, unfortunately, had no proof at my command. I was court-martialed and sentenced to be shot. My captors were men who knew me—most of them were my neighbors, and despised me for not having taken sides with them.

The night was intensely cold. Under a tree I lay, bound with a rope. There were no tents; the command was under marching orders. There were no fires; there was nothing but gloom and a freezing atmosphere. One of my guards was a man who owned a small farm near mine. I had done him favors.

"Mills," said I—he was standing near me—"Mills, this war business is very serious, isn't it?"

"It is for traitors," he answered.

" That's all right, Mills; but you shouldn't talk that

way to me simply because I held an opinion opposite to your own."

"My opinion is the one held by the State," he replied. "You must remember that Kentucky didn't go out of the Union. Therefore, you are not only a traitor to the general government, but a traitor to your own commonwealth."

"You look at it that way, and perhaps you are right, but I was born in Virginia and Virginia has gone out. I am inclined to believe that we made a mistake. As for myself, I should hate to see this country disrupted."

"Yes, it seems so," he sarcastically answered. "The certainty of being shot at daylight has a tendency to make a man thoughtful at midnight."

"Mills."

"Well; but don't talk so loud. You are supposed to keep silent; but what were you going to say?"

"I was going to say that I dont want to be shot at daylight."

"Oh, you were. How did so strange a thought occur to you?"

"It occurred to me in a most natural way. Now, just change places with me and—"

"No, thank you."

"I mean that you just suppose yourself in my fix."

"My imagination isn't that strong. At school, you know, I was always a matter-of-fact sort of fellow. You were the imaginative boy of the class."

"Yes, and that's one of the reasons why I don't relish the idea of being shot at daybreak. It strikes me that if I were in your position and you in mine, I would do something for you."

"Oh, yes, when a man's fancy is wrought up, as yours must be, anything is likely to strike him."

"Mills, don't you remember that if it hadn't been for my father your brother might have gone to the penitentiary?"

"Yes; but what's that got to do with this affair?"

"I should think that gratitude would arise and answer that question."

"That was very well said, but you must know that gratitude rarely keeps a man from being shot at sunrise. I gad, it rarely keeps him from starving to death. There is no gratitude, captain."

"There may not be with some people."

"I mean that no man is grateful enough to risk his life. But before you go any farther, let me say that it would have been better had that brother of mine gone to the pen."

"Why?"

"Well, he's in the rebel army."

"Mills," I said, after a few moment's silence, "if it

were not for one thing, to-morrow morning could not strike so great a terror to my heart."

"What's that?"

"I am engaged to marry Mary Caldwell."

"Handsome girl, but she'll soon forget you."

"I wish I were untied."

"Yes, I reckon you would like to take to your heels."

"I would run away, but not until I had knocked you down."

"Good boy; but I reckon you'd better stop talking now and go to sleep. You want to be in good trim, you know, for the devil's dress parade."

He walked off a short distance and sat down, I imagined, for I could not see. I wondered what time it was, and just then I heard Mills say, in answer to an inquiry, that it must be about four o'clock. I heard something move on the ground near me, and then there came a whisper that thrilled my heart:

"Doan say er word, Mars George—I'se yere."

Then I felt myself slowly dragged, and then I was lifted from the ground and carefully carried away in the deepened darkness of the thick woods.

"Does you know me?" came another whisper.

"Yes; God bless you."

"Hush. Let me git you round on my back an' den we'll be all right."

He seemed to be running, especially after he struck

a path, and shortly afterwards the raking boughs of the trees assured me that we were again in the thick woods.

"Put me down and untie me," I whispered.

"Hush."

He hastened along, going faster and faster. He crossed a frozen stream and began to climb a hill.

"I can put you down now," he said, after a long time. He put me down and cut the rope that bound me. I was so stiff and sore that I could scarcely walk.

The grayish advance of dawn was marching down the hillside when we halted. Old Amos turned to me. Again there was the sudden gleam of an ivory smile.

"Mars George, I forgibs you, sah, fur not makin' me er present o' dat 'possum dog. You gib me ez er Chris'mas present er freedom what de Lawd has permitted me ter enjoy; and now, sah, on dis Chris'mas mawnin——"

"This is Christmas, Amos; I had not thought of it."

"Yas, an' I gives you yo' freedom ez er present. You'll find er hoss in dat little stable down yander, sah. Good bye, and may de Lawd bless you."

OLD JOBLEY.

OLD JOBLEY was always accompanied by a deaf and dumb boy, his grandson. The only word the boy could utter and, so far as any one could discover, the only word he could hear was " Zib." Sometimes, and particularly at early morning when he felt disposed to be loquacious, he would run up to the old man and cry " zib, zib, zib." Then it was known that he was moved by the cheering influences of the season, or that the currents of his small and silent life were smooth and of pleasant gliding.

What a drunkard old man Jobley was! Yes, so much of a drunkard that people said that had he not wasted his life with drink he surely would have gone to Congress. What a fallacy. A man of an ordinary mind gets drunk and says foolish things that are sudden enough and strange enough to be interesting, and people say that liquor is at its old trick of blighting a great intellect. Jobley was a man of pretty fair sense, it is true, and though he might have gone to Congress —for many shadowy minds have gone thither—yet he could not have become a statesman, even though there never had been distilled a drop of anything that would make a man forget his dignity. But how he did like to sit around and talk about what he would have been had he never drunk liquor ; and he always made it out that he surely would have been rich.

During his whole life he had lived on a hillside farm, and from what source his riches could have come no one in the community was sufficiently imaginative to surmise. The old man was a periodical debaucher, and whenever he got off a spree he invariably declared it to be his last.

"I simply won't waste my life in any such a way," he would declare. "I do quit for five months at a time, and a man that can quit that long can quit forever. Just watch me, now; you just keep your eye on the old man and he'll show you what firmness is. Won't he Zib?"

"Zib, zib," the boy would reply.

When the old fellow was getting well after a spree, the boy always took care of him. The old man's wife had no patience with such ailments.

"He needn't expect me to wait on him," she would say. "Heaven knows I was worn out with him years and years ago. He ruined my life, gracious knows. It's a good thing that poor little child don't understand things, but how he can love an old drunkard is more than I can see."

"If you had been more patient with him years ago he might not have been so bad," a privileged neighbor once remarked. "There is such a thing as curing a man by gentleness. I know that my George used to get drunk, but I shamed him out of it before it took much of a hold on him. I didn't scold him—I treated him so kindly that his conscience kept him sober."

"Oh you needn't talk to me about conscience. A drunkard hasn't got any."

"After a while may be not, but he has at first. I know that my George used to suffer awfully in mind, and when I'd come into the room he'd seem to be afraid to look at me—afraid I'd scold him—but I wouldn't let on that I thought he'd done wrong. You ought to have tried that plan, for I believe that many a man has been saved that way."

"That's all nonsense. The whippin' post is the thing."

"Well, I've tried that plan and you haven't, and my husband is a sober man and yours isn't. That's all I've got to say. Good day."

Seven months had passed and old Jobley was still sober. One evening, sitting by the log fire with Zib on his knee, he spoke of his long period of abstinence.

"It's nothin' to boast about," his wife said, shaking a cat out of a chair and sitting down. "Seven months indeed! My father was never drunk in his life, and here you brag because you've been sober seven months."

"No, I'm not exactly braggin', mother, but I'm sorter congratulatin' myself."

"Well, you'd better not holler till you get out of the woods."

"No use to holler at all then, Martha. But if you holler before you get out of the woods somebody may come and help you out. How's that Zib?"

The boy did not look up and the old man shouted "Zib!" and the boy looked up quickly and replied, "Zib, Zib."

At the breakfast table the next morning the old man said:

"Martha, me and Zib are goin' out to the post office this mornin' for I believe there must be a letter for us. Heigh?"

"You don't believe nothin' of the sort. You just want to go there and get drunk; that's exactly what you want, or you wouldn't go such a cold, snowy day as this."

"There you go," the old man replied; "you are the most suspicious creature I ever saw in my life. Why, if I was as suspicious as you I wouldn't believe— wouldn't believe the Bible, even. Let me tell you one thing right here; there ain't money enough in this county to put a drop of liquor in me. Do you understand? Not money enough in this whole county. I'm goin' out there, and if there ain't no letter for me I'm comin' right straight back. Now mark what I tell you —right straight back."

Off they went on the roan mare—the gray old man and the deaf and dumb boy. The day was intensely cold, with a spiteful spitting of snow. A log fire crackled in the back room of the general store and post office, and a loud company was gathered there. Old Jobley, with the boy on his knee, sat for a time listening to the stories he had often heard before. "Lem," he said, speaking to the postmaster, "it struck me last night that there must be a letter here for me."

"Why, who on earth would waste time a writin' to you?" Pud Perdue cried.

"Never mind about that, Pud," the old man answered. "Bet I get ten letters to your one."

"Bet neither one of you never did get ten letters," a red-eyed fellow shouted.

"That's neither here nor there," said the old man. "I 'lowed last night there was a letter here for me, and I wish you'd see if there is, Lem."

"No use lookin', Jobley, for I know there ain't," Lem replied.

"Well, then, I reckon about all I've got to do is to go home."

"Oh, don't be snatched," said the red-eyed fellow, "we're goin' to open a kag of nails in a minit."

"You can go home when you can't go nowhere else," Lem remarked with a quotation from the time-honored lore of the backwoods.

"Yes, I guess that's so, but I told the old woman I'd be right back."

"And of course she knowed you were lyin'," said Pud.

"Sorter seemed like she did," the old man replied. "Say, boys, it has been seven months since I touched a drop."

"Oh, come now," Lem protested.

"Yes, I'll swear to it. Seven months; and it strikes me that a man ought to gather up pretty good control of himself in that length of time."

"Seems like he ought," said the red-eyed fellow.

"There are times," remarked the old man, "when a little liquor does a man a heap of good."

"I reckon you're right."

"Say, Lem, draw us off some in that pint cup."

* * * * * *

When old Mrs. Jobley, after an anxious night of waiting, opened the door at early morning, she saw the roan mare, with snow on her back, standing at the gate.

The neighbors turned out to search the woods, and

at noontime they came upon the old man lying in the snow; and the boy was crouched down beside him, with his face hidden in the folds of his grandfather's coat. They saw at once that the old fellow was dead. A man touched the little fellow and cried :

"Zib!"

But the child did not look up.

OLD BILLY.

Rain came in dashes. It was like the angry spitting of a cornered cat. The landscape was dreary; the farmhouses seemed as blotches of wretchedness—the train roared toward Chicago. There were not many passengers. Some of them were nodding, others sat in gloomy resignation, but there were three men who were inclined to be prankish. These three men, Brooks, Adams and Cooper, were actually laughing, at one of the oldest of jokes, doubtless, and a gaunt old fellow, wise enough to be miserable, was frowning on them in sour disapproval when the train stopped at a station. A woman, with a bundle almost as large as a feather bed, bumped her way off, and a comical-looking old fellow nodded and " ducked " his way on. What a peculiar old fellow he did appear to be, with his squinting eyes set so close together and with his hook-nose shaped so much like a scythe. His type is not found in old countries—quiet self assurance in homespun clothes exists only in America.

" What have we picked up now ? " said Brooks.

" The governor of the state, perhaps," Adams answered, and then added: "Cooper, go and ask that old fellow to explain himself."

"Well, I don't know that he owes me an explanation," Cooper replied, "but if you say so I'll go and tell him that you want to see him."

"All right, go and tell him to come down here and make himself sociable."

Cooper told the old fellow that he was wanted, and he good humoredly came back and joined the friends.

"You looked lonesome up there," said Brooks, "and we didn't know but you might be willing to enter into a sort of reciprocity with us."

"Much obleeged," the old fellow replied, squinting comically.

"Where are you from?" Adams asked.

"Wall," he answered, pulling at his thin, streaky beard, "my home is down yan in Kaintucky, sah. Come up here in Indiany to see my married daughter that lives back yander a piece. Hearn her husband wa'n't treatin' her very well and I 'lowed, I did, that I'd come up and maul him awhile. I transacted my business with him and I reckon it's all right now."

"What's your name?"

"Old Billy."

"Which way are you going now?" Cooper asked.

"Thiser way," he answered, pointing forward.

"Yes, so I see."

"Glad of it, sah. I'm always glad to l'arn that a person aint blind. I 'lowed I'd go up here to Chicago and see how all them rascals are gittin' along. Rascals tickle me might'ly."

"There isn't fun enough in this," Brooks adroitly whispered, and then said aloud: "Well, Old Billy you say you live in Kentucky?"

"Yes, sah, in Allen county."

"Well, then, tell us a story. I have heard that Allen county is full of yarns."

"I don't know any story. You don't know Ab Starbuck, do you?"

"No; but what about him?"

"Nothin', only he was about the toughest man in Kaintucky. And mean! Thar wa'n't nuthin' too mean for him to do. One night over on Big Sandy he rid into a meetin' house durin' a revival and shot out the lights and left the mourners thar in the dark. Oh, he was bad, and when he got on the rampage folks had to git out of his way. When he come to town business jest nachully suspended. I never shall furgit one day when he come to Scottville. A good many of the merchants closed their doors when they hearn that he had come, and men were pretty scarce on the street, I tell you. Wall, Ab he come a stalkin' along the sidewalk with a couple of pistols in his belt, and a bowie knife in his boot leg. Old men got out of his way, and little children got off the sidewalk down in the mud to let him pass. Wall, jest about the time he was the worst lookin'—jest atter he had kicked a dog out into the street, here come an old nigger man, walkin' along, meetin' him. The nigger didn't git out of the way—he walked right into Ab Starbuck—bumped against him. Ab jumped back. He was too much astonished to think about his bowie knife, and he hauled off with his monstrus fist and hit the nigger in the mouth. The old man staggered. He wiped his bloody lips with one hand, and began to feel about at arm's length in front of him with the other; and then, in a voice as gentle as a child's, he said:

"'Boss, you must skuze me, sah; I'se blind.'

"'My God, old man! I didn't know that!' Ab cried, and then stood with his hand restin' on the nigger's shoulder. 'Old man,' he said, 'I wouldn't hurt you for the world,' and he took out his hankerchief and wiped the nigger's lips. 'Old man,' he went on, 'that hat you've got on aint fit to wear. Come in here,' and he led him into a store that happened not to be closed up on account of the desperado. 'Here,' he called, and the storekeeper began to dance around, 'give this old man the best hat you've got in the house. W'y, your shoes are all worn out, too, old man. We'll jest get a new pair, that's what we'll do. And you need a coat too. Oh, we can't afford to go around lookin' shabby. We don't care what it costs. Here, young fellow, hustle around. Hand us a coat.' He stood lookin' on with tender eyes. When the nigger was rigged out, Ab asked:

"'Whar was you headed for, old gentleman—and God knows you are a gentleman, I don't care how black you are.'

"'I was goin' down to the wagin yard, sah.'

"'Wall, it's too muddy to walk down thar with them new shoes on, so I'll jest send you down thar in a hack. Here, Mister, make out your bill'; and when he had paid what was due the store he put the old man in a hack and sent him away."

The three friends looked at one another but said nothing. The train stopped at a station, and a tired-looking woman, carrying a little girl in her arms, got on. She took a seat just opposite the three friends and Old Billy. The little girl began to cry. Brooks bought her an orange, but she would not take it. Adams offered her an apple, but she screamed at him.

"Oh, I don't know what to do with her," said the woman, sighing. "I don't know what is the matter with her."

Old Billy looked at the woman and then at the child. "Your child, madam?" he asked.

"Yes, sir."

"Your only child, I reckon."

"Yes, sir."

"The only one you've ever had, I take it."

"Well, yes, sir," she answered, regarding him curiously.

"And you were an only child, too, I reckon."

"I was, sir."

"And you didn't play with children much."

"No, sir."

"I thought not."

The old man got up, took a little shawl that had been thrown on a seat, twisted it, tied a knot at one end, smoothed the thing into the semblance of a rag doll, handed it to the little girl and said: "Love the doll." The little creature seized the rag and hugged it. She ceased crying in a moment, and in a sweet disregard of what was going on about her, hummed the improvised tune of tenderness.

"Madam," said the old man, "your little girl simply wanted somethin' to love and protect."

"Gentlemen," Brooks remarked, arising, "the man who can thus touch the earliest bud of woman's noble nature—the very germ of the truest of all affection, motherly love, is my master. He is not Old Billy, but, gentlemen, he is the Hon. William."

SWINGING IN THE DUSK.

The Hatchie river was raging. Far away over the hills black clouds were hanging, and dogwood trees, still green of leaf and white of blossom, came down the tumbling stream. The air was warm and heavy, and the woodpecker that flew over the bottom field appeared likely to fall ere he could reach the dead tree that stood at the edge of the clearing. Reports from up the river gave exciting accounts of another swell coming down from the mountains, and in the neighborhood of Hickory Flat there was nothing talked of except the disasters of the flood. A yoke of oxen belonging to old Matt Sprague had been dumped out of a lot by the sudden caving of a bank and whirled away, and it was excitingly reported that a fine brood mare, the property of 'Squire Nickelson, had been washed against a tree and killed. The Hatchie was a treacherous stream, and the people had been brought up in the belief that it could be guilty of almost any trick known to the southern tributaries of the Mississippi, but no one had been sufficiently schooled to suspect this stream capable of so broad-spread a disaster as was now threatened.

Lit Halpin, a hard-working fellow who had married one of the Lanier girls, had just completed a one-story board house in the second bottom of the Hatchie. At the time of his marriage he was a hired man on a farm; and a hired man in that part of the country is scarcely a Ward McAllister of society. But the knowledge that there existed a prejudice against him did not seem to lie with much weight upon the mind of Lit Halpin. He said that he wasn't much of a society man anyway; declared that he didn't care to ride about on Sundays wearing high-heeled boots that were too small for him —and this the social life of Hickory Flat imperiously demanded—he sought simply an opportunity to earn a living. And he did earn a living. Not only this, he won the love of the handsomest girl in the community in an accidental way and married her. He bought a piece of land in the rich second bottom and had just put away his tools, after completing his modest house, when the Hatchie began its threatening rise.

"Allie," he said, speaking to his wife, "I believe the old Hatch is going to try to gouge us out. Up a little way from here it is digging pretty sharply into the bank."

"Oh, I hope not, Lit." She was standing on the veranda.

"So do I, but that won't keep the water back. If hope worked half the time there wouldn't be one-third as much trouble in the world."

"That's true," she admitted; and after a moment's silence, she asked:

"Do you think we can do anything?"

"Not much." He turned and looked about him. "Allie," said he, "I'll tell you what we might do. We might tie the house with a cable rope, so that if the water does come we'll be anchored."

"Oh, that would be charming," she cried. "But will it float?" she asked, becoming serious.

"Of course it will. I'll go and get that well rope and fix the thing right now."

The rope was found to be long enough. He attached one end to the strong underpinning of the house, and the other end he made fast to a large cottonwood tree, leaving a play of about fifty feet. He smiled at his own ingenuity, and said that if the freakish river should take a turn in his direction, it would find him prepared. Just then a man rode up.

"Lit," he called, "the water is about to sweep old man Potts from the face of the earth. We must go down and help him save his cattle. Here, hop up behind me."

This admitted of no protest, nor of a moment's questioning. Lit jumped upon a stump and sprang upon the horse.

"Allie," he called, looking back, "stay in the house and you'll be all right. There's no danger, anyway, but stay in the house."

The horse galloped away. The woman went about her work. The clouds over the hills grew darker but the sun shone on the house, and in the brightness there was so blithe a promise that the danger would pass that the wife hummed a tune as she worked. Suddenly there came a roar and a jar. She ran out upon the veranda. The river had cut through the field. The house was afloat. The current was swift, and the rope was taut. There was no way to reach land, and the woman, feeling that she was safe, sat down to await the return of her husband. Some one called her, and looking up she saw a man standing near the tree at the other end of the rope.

"Where's Lit?" the man asked.

"Gone to help save cattle. And why don't you go to help, too. You ought to be ashamed of yourself, Tobe."

The man looked about him. "Yes," he said, "but there are other things in this life that a person might be ashamed of. I know people that ought to be ashamed of something worse than not saving cattle.

I know a woman who promised to marry a man and didn't."

"Go on away, Tobe; I don't want to have any words with you."

"Don't you? But I reckon you will."

"If Lit were here you wouldn't talk to me that way. I'm going to tell him when he comes home."

The water was so loud in its roar that she had to lift her voice.

"Do you reckon?" he shouted. "When do you expect to see him again?"

"He'll be home pretty soon—too soon for your good."

"Do you think so?"

"If I had something to shoot with you shouldn't stand there and torment me."

"Do you reckon? You ought to have kept your gun at home instead of letting folks borrow it. Say, after you fooled me I told you that you'd be sorry, didn't I?"

"I didn't fool you, Tobe."

"Yes, you did; you said you'd marry me."

"Well, but I told you shortly afterward that I couldn't. That wasn't fooling you."

"Wasn't it? I think it was, and I told you that you'd be sorry. You couldn't keep your word, but I'm going to show you that I can keep mine. The water's swift out there, ain't it?"

"What do you mean to do!" she cried in alarm.

"I'm going to keep my word."

"Tobe, please go on away."

"I will—I'll go one way and you'll go another. The water's pretty swift out there, ain't it?"

"What are you doing?" she shrieked. "For God's sake don't cut that rope, Tobe!"

The house went whirling down the stream.

CHAPTER II.

IN a remote community, near the line of the Indian territory, a rude court sat in session. A prisoner, tied with a rope, sat on a bench. He had come into the neighborhood six months before, and had killed a man. Now he was on trial for his life. The verdict was brought in, and just then a man strode into the room.

"Judge," he said, "wait a moment. I'm no lawyer and have no right to talk in court, but I beg you to listen to me."

"This is a court of justice rather than of law," the judge answered. "Speak."

The prisoner drew back and tried to hide his face.

"Gentlemen," said the man who had just entered, "for months I have been looking for the wretch you've got tied there. Listen." He told an affecting story of a home in Tennessee. He told of a flood, and of his house, tied to a tree. He drew a rude but strong picture of his wife sitting on the veranda, with the waters of a mad river roaring about her. "This wretch came up and stood on the bank, gentlemen," he continued. "He declared that my wife had promised to marry him. He knew that I was nowhere about the place—he knew that I had gone to help his own father save his cattle from drowning. Gentlemen, this scoundrel cut the rope that held the house, and—I found her," he added after a pause —"I found her when the river fell. And now I tell you that this hound does not belong to your law, but to mine. See here, I have brought this all the way from Tennessee." He unwound a rope from about his body. "I say he is mine. Judge, did you hear what I said?"

"Mr. Sheriff," said the judge, "we have made a mistake. The prisoner does not belong to us."

Near the place where the court met, a tree leaned over the road, and when evening was come a man sat with his back against a stump, watching a human figure, swinging in the dust.

A MEMORABLE MEAL.

It was at luncheon, and one of Chicago's largest merchants was in a talkative mood. "One particular meal lives in my memory," said he. "It was years ago, and I had just arrived in Chicago. I had come from the East, and had 'worked' my way on canal boats and afterwards hoofed it over the prairie. I had been led to believe that all one had to do was to come here and pick up money. I looked about with an eager eye, but didn't find any. Indeed, I must have struck the town when its pulse was low for I couldn't get any work. I had gone two days with nothing to eat. Something had to be done. I didn't want to steal. In fact, nothing was left lying in my way. But I had to get something to eat, one way or another. I shuddered at the thought of begging, but I stepped into a store and hinted that I should like to eat something. A man looked up from his desk, flashed a measurement over me, and said: 'Get out, you hulk.' For a short time anger relieved my hunger, but resentment, while it may temporarily turn the edge of appetite, can not shut the knife. I was walking along Lake street when the richest of perfume, the fragrance of a New England boiled dinner, came through a doorway. I stepped into the place. At that time it was the largest restaurant in Chicago. A feeling of desperate boldness came over me, and with a firm step I walked back and took a seat at a table. My first intention was to give a modest order, but could modesty serve a thief, and surely I was a thief, for I had come in to steal my dinner. No, I would suffer no self-restraint If I had to steal, I would steal the best. The waiter came and I ordered nearly everything on the bill of fare. It was an eternity before the order was filled, and when it came I was so nervously eager that I could scarcely eat; but after a while I settled down to a sort of physical happiness. No one noticed that I was eating like a wolf. Suddenly a sore dread fell upon me. How was I going to get out? I looked toward the door, and for the first time I noticed that the cashier was a most threatening and burly-looking fellow. Then I began to speculate as to the particular method he would choose to rid me of my life. At last I settled upon the belief that he would kick me to death. This was suggested, I remember, by the fact that just as I sat looking at him he came out from behind the counter and kicked at a dog. Yes, my time had come. I had saved myself from starving merely to die a more violent death. I philosophized that after all life was not worth living. But I was young, and it was hard to die without having accomplished anything. I took up the check which the waiter had placed on the table. Gracious alive, I owed $1.40! I thought of my home, away back in the hills of New England. I thought of my husky father, and I wished that I had his strength. There was no use of putting it off. Better die and get it off my mind. I took the check, walked up to the cashier's desk, and with hopelessness settled into a resignation that might have been taken for the serenest of confidence, I placed the piece of paper in front of that frowning giant. He turned it over, looked at it and then looked at me.

"'Was everything all right?' he asked.

"'Yes, sir.'

"'Well!'

"I looked at him a moment and then said: 'I won't tell a pitiful tale. I was hungry; I had no money; I came in, ordered the best you've got, and now I am at your service.'

"He opened the showcase. Ah! instead of kicking me to death, he was going to shoot me. He reached in and grabbed up something, and, withdrawing his hand, said, 'Have a cigar?'

"That was a long time ago," the merchant continued, after a pause, "but I think of it nearly every time I go into a restaurant. What did you say? Oh, what became of the burly fellow? He is the manager of our wholesale department."

A DEAD MARCH.

At night they brought a man to the hotel. He had sprung up from an opium dream—wild and a maniac. He had gone to a Chinese opium den and for hours he lay in a stupor, but suddenly he awoke with a cry and he sprang up and shook in a frenzy. Some one said that he was staying at a hotel in the "down town" district, and thither they took him. His eyes looked like glass marbles with curiously-wrought figures in them, but the design of the figures could not be traced. They took him to a room and compelled him to lie down. A doctor came and injected morphine into his arm. Some one remarked: "I warrant you he's a handsome fellow when he's at himself."

Three children were playing in the corridor, and a boy, early in beginning the lordly deception which the male feels that it is legitimate to practice on the opposite sex, said to a girl: "He is a robber and they brought him out of a cave where there's ever so much gold, and they're going to kill him."

At intervals during the night the man slept, but at times he would spring up and rave like a demon.

"They are gone, they are murdered," he kept on repeating. "Why didn't they take me. They are murdered."

To a certain class of human beings the following day will ever be memorable. A procession marched along the street. The music was a dead march, but from further down the line came the strains of Annie Laurie. There were coffins with red flags thrown over them. The air was cold and raw, and everywhere there seemed to be a suppressed excitement—a hushed yell. On the sidewalks rough men stood, breathing hard. They were panting for revenge. A man stepped from the throng. He unfurled an American flag, took the lead of the procession and defiantly marched onward. There was a loud murmur—a growl, but no one dared molest him.

A party of ladies and gentlemen were assembled in the drawing-room of the hotel to which the opium maniac had been taken. The procession was passing. Some one accidentally struck the keys of a piano. The next moment the maniac rushed into the room. He had been asleep, and his attendant had left him. The piano had called him back to wakefulness but not to reason. His eyes glared. The designs in them could now have been traced, a man said—coffins with red rags over them.

"They have tried to keep me from it, but they

can't," he cried. "I was born to play their 'funeral march.'"

He threw himself at the piano. A storm arose, and out of the storm came a cry of distress. The storm deepened and there was a rumble as if a great multitude were threatening vengeance. The company turned from the windows and gazed in awe at the pianist. There was present a man who was celebrated in Europe as a musical genius and he was enraptured.

"This is not a man," he cried. "It is a tormented soul."

The procession passed. The strains of "Annie Laurie" were heard far down the street. The storm also had passed, and the piano seemed a green bank where waters rippled. Birds were singing. The ripple grew fainter—the birds were hushed. Silence. The man leaned forward. His nurse ran into the room. The European genius said, "Don't disturb him. He will play again."

They waited, but he did not move. Yes, he did move—He leaned back slowly and fell on the floor. The designs were no longer in his eyes—they may have been there, but the lights were turned out behind them.

His name was never discovered. He had registered when he came to the hotel, but when the book was examined there was found an unintelligible scratch.

AN IMPERIOUS COURT.

Negley was riding along a road in a remote and picturesque part of southern Missouri. The day was delightful—the weather had crossed the imaginary line that fancy has drawn between Spring and Summer. Negley did not belong to any temperance order, or if he did his adherence to its precepts was not very strict, for as he rode along there in the sunshine he took out a whisky bottle, held it up and looked through it. That hasty survey assured him that there was but one drink left.

"Well, I might as well take it off my mind and put it where it will do more good or harm," he mused. "What's this," he added, looking at a line of print across the label on the flask. "'Please break this bottle.' Now why should I put myself to that trouble? My obligation ended when I paid for the stuff, and the manufacturer has no more right to make any further demand. But after all it's a very slight request. It implies but little exertion on my part." He drank the whisky and again looked at the request. This time he noticed it was printed in red. "All right, gentlemen, I will go you," said he, and rising in his stirrups he threw the bottle at a rail fence. The bottle whirled through an opening, made by a crooked rail, and then there came a loud cry like the howl of a wild beast. And a man jumped up, looked about him, sprang over the fence, and, bounding to the middle of the road, in front of Negley, shook his fist and exclaimed:

"So I've got you. Oh, attempt to get away and I'll shoot the top of your head off. Can't lie down to take a little nap but somebody must come along and try to kill me. But I've got you."

"My dear sir," said Negley, "I humbly beg your pardon. I didn't see you until after I had thrown that bottle."

"You didn't, hay? Haven't you got anything to do but go about the country throwing bottles? What did you throw at if you didn't throw at me? Oh, I've got you!"

"My dear sir, I threw at the fence."

"What did you want to throw at the fence for? And do you mean to tell me that you couldn't hit that fence? And say, Why did you want to hit the fence?"

"I wanted to break the bottle."

"What did you want to break the bottle for? Why couldn't you have thrown it over there against that rock? Look here, your aim was to assassinate one of the most prominent citizens of this neighborhood, and if any law can be squeezed out of the statutes of this State you shall suffer for it. Turn off yonder at the right, and ride slowly toward that house across the creek."

"Look here," Negley protested, "you can't arrest me without a warrant."

"Can't I? We'll see. Things may be different where you came from, but in this part of the country the law doesn't sit cross-legged and see a criminal get away just because no warrant has been issued for him. Ride on, there."

Negley is a peaceable sort of a fellow, and he is also a man of exquisite judgment; so he rode along. When he arrived at the gate in front of the house that had been pointed out, he was told to dismount. He did so, and just then a girl, swift of motion and with a wild tangle of dark hair, came out.

"Hal," said Negley's captor, "here's a fellow that tried to kill me just now, and I'm going to have him tried for his life, even if we do have to stretch a point in law. Here, take this pistol and hold him here until I come back."

The girl took the pistol and the man disappeared. "What is he going to do?" Negley asked.

"He's gone after the constable and the clerk. Got

to have 'em or he can't run the court. He's the Judge."

"Look here, miss, I didn't hit your father intentionally. I simply threw a bottle away to break it and happened to hit him."

"Was there anything in the bottle?" she asked.

"No."

"Then no wonder he got mad."

Negley's face brightened. "And won't you please let me ride on away?"

"No, I'll have to keep you till pap comes."

"But you could shoot at me and not hit me."

"Oh, hitting you wouldn't make so much difference, but I might hit the horse, and that would be bad."

She held him there until the old man returned, and then a formal indictment was issued. The Judge decided that the case was not bailable, and it was therefore necessary to keep the prisoner in close confinement until the next day, when it was intended that the trial should begin. So the prisoner was locked in the smokehouse and a guard was appointed. Negley sat down on a box of salt pork and cursed the backwoods institutions of his country. He knew that he could have the old man arrested and severely dealt with, but that was small consolation. What he wanted was to get out of that greasy prison.

"Who's on guard out there?" he asked, talking through a crack.

"I am."

"Oh, is that you, miss?"

"Yes. Jim, the constable, has gone to get something to eat and I have to stay until he gets back."

"What time of night is it?"

"'Bout ten, I think."

"Look here, if you will let me out I will send you a silk dress."

"I'd like to have one powerful but I have to do my duty. Here comes Jim."

The next day Negley was arraigned before what purported to be a solemn court. The old man presided with severe dignity. He not only pointed out the crime of striking a man with a bottle, but declared that added to this crime was the awful offense of contempt of court, as he himself was the man who had received the blow. The prisoner urged that out of the tender obedience of his nature he had simply obeyed a request pasted on a bottle. But the bottle was produced. The label was gone—some evil-minded person had removed it. This was a serious complication. "Prisoner," said the Judge, "I don't see but one way out of it. Marry the girl."

"What!" the prisoner exclaimed.

"Yes, that's the law. You become my son-in-law or take the consequences."

This appeared to satisfy the entire court. The prisoner, who had been watching for an opportunity, darted through the doorway, tumbled over a fence and was soon in a woods. He had left a fine horse, but he had escaped a wife. Several weeks later, while sitting in a St. Louis hotel, Negley overheard the following fragment of a conversation: "Yes, I was down in that country once and was arrested on some fool charge—don't exactly remember now what it was—and the court decided that I should marry a girl. The girl had nothing to do with the affair, but that made no difference. Well, I seized what I thought to be an accidental opportunity and ran away, leaving a $250 horse. I afterward heard that this was the aim of the court. I hear that other men have been trapped pretty much in the same way."

HIS SPECIAL.

THERE lived in Chicago, not long ago, an old fellow whom the newspaper men knew as old Marcus. He was known in all the newspaper offices; he haunted them at most inopportune times when the city editor was on the stretcher of a threatened "scoop" and when the night editor was on the frenzied tiptoe of closing the "forms." Old Marcus always had an important "special" to sell, "just for enough to get along on." Want had made him weazen; poverty had slapped him into servility of manner, but he aspired to write on monetary subjects. The antennæ of his mind were constantly feeling for some financial crisis. He knew exactly how many dollars there were in the government vaults; he could tell you how many dollars were appropriated by the late session of congress, and could recite, with astonishing glibness, page after page from the *Banker's Monthly.* An ordinary event did not interest him. He would not read even the headlines of a sensational murder, but would hungrily gulp down the details of a bank failure. On the night after the Bladridge murder he went into the office of a morning paper and shrinking his way to the city editor's desk, said :

"Mr. Lowery, pardon my interruption, but I have a very strong article here that I wish you'd look at. The shipment of gold from this country——"

The city editor wheeled about and gave him a look that jolted him. "Great Cæsar, Marcus, this is no time to talk about shipments of gold. We'd have no room to-night for an account of the discovery of Capt. Kidd's boodle; we've got a great murder on hand—a magnificent murder. Why don't you go to the news editor with your stuff. It's not in my line anyway."

"He won't talk to me—doesn't seem to know what he wants. Now, on the sixteenth there was shipped from New York, $3,562,840, and——"

"That'll do. Gracious alive, how your head must ache, trying to keep up with all that stuff."

"But it is of extreme importance to the country."

"Of course. Why don't you take it to a financial paper?"

"Because a man has to be a banker or the average financial paper won't pay any attention to him."

"Well, so long, Marcus. I haven't time to talk to you to-night. Go and find out who killed Bladridge and reap the reward of a scoop."

"I am no detective, Mr. Lowery."

"That's all right. So long."

"There'll be a time, Mr. Lowery, when you'll be glad to get the first whack at something I write."

"I hope so."

"I'll furnish you an item one of these days that'll wake you up."

"All right, but put it off as long as you can."

The old man fumbled his way down the stairs and went to another newspaper office. The city editor was in a stew and the night editor was boiling. They snapped at him when he offered his special. He went away and sought his room up a dark and ill-smelling alley. The place was miserable. Its atmosphere was heavy with the steamy stench of a midnight lunch, served in a neighboring hell-hole. The old man lighted a lamp and placed it on a goods box which served as a desk. There was no furniture in the room, except a stool-bottom chair with the back broken off, and a few cooking utensils. Newspaper cuttings, containing numerous figures and dollar marks, were tacked here and there on the wall, as if they were gems in oil, holding a rich bit of landscape or a handsome face.

Old Marcus sat down with a weary and discouraged drop. He sat for a time, seeming to be worn out, and then, taking up his pen, began to write. Suddenly his old and wrinkled face flushed, and his form rounded out. His hastening pen left an enchanting track of figures. He mumbled over them and mur-

mured, "beautiful," as if he were a poet, astonished at the wasteful outpour of his own inspiration.

"Seventy-six millions, nine hundred and four thousand, six hundred and fourteen," he muttered. "Beautiful, and yet they won't take it; but they will take something one of these days. I will thrill them."

CHAPTER II.

One Sunday night Lowery looked up to find old Marcus standing near.

"Helloa, Marcus."

"Good evening, Mr. Lowery. Are you pushed for time?"

"Never pushed much Sunday night; but say, don't tell me anything about the financial condition of the country. I never did have time enough to hear about that."

"But I have a thing here that would be the very thing for Monday morning. Now, Wall street—"

"Great Cæsar, Marcus, don't begin that. Don't you get tired? Say, you ought to go off somewhere and rest; you can't stand the strain much longer. There is nothing that wears harder on the brain than financiering, and you'd better look out. Don't you know that Gould and all those fellows have been warned by their physicians, not to keep up the strain too long? Look out, Marcus."

"Mr. Lowery," said the old man, and in his voice there was a tone of sadness, "I am too old and too feeble to be made fun of this way. I know you don't mean any harm by it, and for a long time I could stand it, but I have been so oppressed of late that what was once a mere reminder that I was carrying something has become a heavy load. Don't make fun of me."

Lowery had shoved back his chair, and was regarding the old man with an expression of sympathy.

"Marcus, you know that I wouldn't say anything to hurt your feelings. I am sorry for you if you are in distress, and will help you out if I can. Where are you from, anyway, old man?"

For the first time he felt a sort of interest in this strange piece of driftwood on the river of life.

"I came from Boston seven years ago. Ah, Lowery," he added with a brightening face, "there's the financial town for you. I used to write for the weekly *Statement*, published there, and the editor often said that he didn't see how he could get along without me. Do you remember, about ten years ago, an article giving an exhaustive account of the debt of England—how she owed more than all the coined money in the world could pay?"

"I read something like that, but I don't know where I saw it," Lowery answered.

"Well, no matter where you saw it, I wrote it."

"Did the editor of the weekly *Statement* pay you for your contributions?"

"Oh, gracious, yes."

"How much?"

"Oh, he used to pay me a dollar a column. It wasn't much, I know, but in these days of dry rot and sensationalism, a man ought to be glad to get the truth printed at almost any price. That reminds me that I have an article here that will create a sensation throughout the country. It involves the sum of forty-eight millions, five hundred——"

"That's enough," Lowery interposed.

"But don't you want the article?"

"No, I'm afraid it's too sensational."

"Nonsense, Lowery. It would add tone and dignity to your paper. I was noticing this morning what a lot of dry stuff you print—not one gleam of light except a few figures telegraphed from Washington."

The city editor made a gesture of impatience. The great financier continued: "Of course, you needn't take it. I didn't expect you would. You are hired to get up news for unthinking people, and a piece of real intelligence is of no use to you. I'll bet that one of these days I'll write an article that you'll want."

"How many millions will it involve?"

"Not a blessed cent."

"Ah, you begin to interest me."

"You'll not only be interested, but thrilled when you see the article."

"When are you going to write it?"

"I don't know exactly, but when you read it you will be astonished at my power to produce sensational matter, and the boys in the office will talk about it, and the whole town will be eager to know more of the writer."

"All right, bring it up."

"No, I shall not bring it."

"You'll send it in, eh?"

"No, I'll not do that, either."

"Then how am I to get it?"

"If you'll give me a dollar I'll promise to direct it to you."

"All right, here's your money."

The old man took the dollar and went out. They heard him fumbling his way down the narrow stairs, and then one of the men said:

"Didn't know you ever paid in advance, Mr. Lowery."

"Poor fellow," replied the city editor, "he needed the dollar. I don't think, however, that he'll need many more."

"I'll bet," said a reporter, "that he'll never furnish an item until he's dead."

Some time passed, and old Marcus did not call, but one night just as some one had mentioned his name, there came a telephone message announcing that he was dead. About an hour later a reporter came in, and handing Lowery a sealed envelope, said: "This was found on old Marcus' desk addressed to you. The police don't know whether he died a natural death or committed suicide. Maybe this will tell."

Lowery tore open the envelope and read the following:

MY SENSATIONAL SPECIAL.

"I told you that I would write you a sensational special. Here it is. I know that I shall not be able to get out of my room again, as it is about as much as I can do to sit up, and I must hasten to the fulfillment of my promise.

"A number of years ago, while I lived in Boston, I did a great deal of writing, as I once told you, for the *Statement*. Once, while in the office, I met a very pleasant man who had just handed in his views on an important financial transaction. We talked a while and I found him to be bright and entertaining. I met him a number of times and became interested in him. One day while we were talking, my wife, who was down town shopping, called for me. I introduced him, and when she and I left the office he accompanied us. We walked some distance together, and when we parted, I gave him the number of our house and asked him to call. He said that he should be pleased to do so, and he did call several evenings later and made himself most agreeable. My wife was a handsome and charming woman, much younger than I. She was much taken with the fellow. You can begin to surmise, can't you? You can, unless you are as stupid as I was. This man called frequently, and instead of keeping up a financial talk with me, talked literature to my wife. Fool is the practical man who marries a woman of literary bent. The fellow of gabbling nonsense, of metrical blubbers, of the dactylic dripping of mental foam, can come along and wind a pliant will about his finger. Babbled literature has ruined many an honest plodder's home. Look at the farmer boy. What a fool he is to marry a girl that loves poetry. Well, one day when I went home I found that my wife had run away with that villain. They had gone, I knew not whither, but I felt within my soul that I should meet them again and kill them. I could not follow them—I was too poor. Some time afterwards I learned that they were in Europe. Then, after a long time, I met a man who told me that my wife was dead and that the man was living in Chicago, that he was wealthy and, consequently, esteemed. I came to Chicago almost as a tramp. The man, I learned, had gone with a party of capitalists to South America. I resolved to wait for him, and I lived on bitter bread and sweet hope. I had a long knife, made of a file and finely tempered. I would kill him with that. Why? One day my wife put a ring—his ring—on her finger and couldn't get it off. 'I will fix it,' he said, and he went to a hardware store and got a file and filed it off. The operation must have been painful, done with the clumsy fingers of love, and the flesh was torn, but she looked up at him and smiled. It was then that I knew he had won her heart. Yes, I would kill him with that knife, but I pawned it to a saloon man, so reduced was I, and he used it to carve beef for the free lunch. One day, while I was standing in the saloon, in walked my man. I stepped back and he did not notice me. He went up to the lunch counter and cut off a piece of beef with my knife—ah, his knife, too—and after taking a drink went away. I tried to raise money enough to get the knife—I wrote financial items but could not sell them. At last I worked for the saloon man; I cleaned out his spittoons and got my knife. Then, every night, I looked for my man. I was cautious, for I didn't want to be hanged. One night, after writing an article which I hoped you would accept, I started for your office. I saw my man. I followed him and I pressed the knife affectionately against me as I walked along. My man turned into an alley, evidently to go to a retired saloon, and I hastened after him. He did go into the saloon and I waited in the alley, not far off. He came out and approached me. I stood against the wall. Should I stab him without saying anything? No. I wanted to hear him speak. I spoke to him and he stopped.

"'Who are you?' he asked.

"'My name is File and Ring,' I said.

"'I never heard of such a fool name.'

"'Then I will introduce myself,' and I stabbed him. He made a smothered noise—and was dead. I pulled my knife out of his breast, wiped it on his beard and hastened to my miserable room. Ah, there was a great sensation the next morning. An enterprising citizen had been murdered, and it was no ordinary murder, for none of the valuables on his person had been molested. The next night I took my financial article to your office and you and your man were talking about my man, and were wondering if the police would catch the murderer. I am the man that killed Bladridge. You will find the knife in my pillow, and if you question the truth of my statement, telegraph to R. J. Biscomb, 4311 State street, Boston, and ask him what he knows about me. He does not know where I am and probably does not suspect that I committed the murder, but will believe what I have written. I have kept my promise—have written a special that will create a sensation. And now I am to die here alone. I could call for help, but need none. Good-bye."

The knife was found in the pillow. A dispatch was sent to R. J. Biscomb, and he replied that he was acquainted with the details of the family trouble through which Marcus had passed, and that the old man had undoubtedly committed the murder.

AT THE SPRING.

In every neighborhood throughout the heavily wooded districts of the South there stands an old log house slowly settling down into decay; and near it, on the same hill, is a white board church. The old house was a place of religious resort years ago, and within its walls America's most fervid oratory was heard. In the fall of the year, when the fodder had been pulled, when the leaves on the oak trees had caught the first breath of autumn, the "revival" began at Mount Zion. A strong man from a distance, a gospel Samson, came to help the young circuit-rider—came to arraign the devil and to paint sin in most horrible colors. Many a shoat was slaughtered, and many a pone of corn bread was baked. Eloquence, zeal, power to convert did not turn the edge of the preacher's appetite. He was a worker and he believed in eating; he gloried in his physical as well as in his religious strength. Indeed, his bodily strength stood him well in hand, for he was sometimes called upon to fight Satan in more forms than one. The tough man from over the creek—and it appeared that the toughest man always lived just across the creek—held preachers in contempt, and was opposed to the spread of the gospel; so the circuit-rider was sometimes forced to get down in the county road, hitch his horse, and thrash this fellow.

As long as the weather was good, the young men remained outside the meeting house, lolling under the trees, talking horse, swapping saddles, knives, and sometimes horses. The old men, the women and the children sat inside, listening to the preacher. The preachers inveighed against this neglect on the part of the young fellows, but it was a custom of the country and could not be remedied. The church was near a spring, and the spring was a place of great social resort. It was here that the young men sat and picked out their future wives from among the young women who dismounted at the horse-block not far away. This is a fair sample of their talk:

"Zeb, how's your tobacco?"

"Putty good. Turning out better than I expected."

"Glad to hear it. I didn't 'low you'd have any. Rid along by your upper patch about a month ago, and a tobacco worm hopped up on the fence and asked me for a chaw; 'lowed he'd dun chawed all yourn up."

This never failed to raise a laugh, even among the old men who had heard it when they were boys.

Once a "revival" was in progress at Oak Grove in Sumner county, Tennessee. It had been a year of great sin, of backsliding, and the new circuit-rider was ambitious to reclaim the swamp lands of the church. And he had made a very fair start. He had wallowed old Sandy Balch in the county road, had larrupped one of the Stallcup boys with an apple tree sprout, and had eaten with marked relish a sweet potato pie baked by the widow Morris. Now all that remained was to persuade the backsliders to return, to urge the new crop of sinners to throw over their evil ways. His only hope to catch the young men was at night; during the day, he must be content with the old men and the women. He was near the close of his sermon, one day at noon; a horse discussion was going on at the spring.

"Now, this horse of mine," said Tom Dabbs, "is one that you read about."

"Yes," Tobe Brock replied, "but this horse of mine is one that men preach about."

"I never hearn nobody preach about him."

"You hain't? Well, you must have paid mighty little attention to the sermon. Brother Hooker is goin' to preach about him to-night."

"Yes, that's mighty fine to tell these folks settin' about here. He's goin' to call up mourners to-night, an' I know he ain't goin' to talk horse."

"He may call up mourners, but he's goin' to talk about my horse, all the same."

"I'll bet you five dollars he don't."

"I've jest got five and I'll take you."

The money was put up; and as Brock was walking away from the spring a friend said: "Tobe, you air mighty foolish to throw away five dollars these hard times."

"Ain't flung away no five dollars."

"Yes, you have, makin' such a bet as that."

"You wait."

The sermon was done and Mr. Hooker was riding toward the place where he was to eat dinner. Tobe Brock overtook him.

"Tobe, why don't you come into the fold?"

"I've been layin' off to do so, Brother Hooker, and I believe I will after a while."

"Why not now, Tobe?"

"Well, I'm breakin' some steers now. Have to wait till I git them broke."

"But what difference does that make?"

"Makes a good deal. No man can break steers without cussin'."

"That's all nonsense."

"Yes, it do look that way to a man that ain't breakin' steers; but let him try it once, and he'll find that cussin' is the nachulest thing in the world. But I am goin' to mend my licks this fall. Say, I've got a little proposition to make to you. Now this fellow, Tom Dabbs—but wait a minute. I heard you say you wanted to fix up the church."

"Yes, I do."

"That's what I thought, and I 'lowed to give you five dollars."

"I wish you would. That would make up the amount."

"I think I can. Now this fellow, Tom Dabbs, thinks a man ain't got courage to do nothin'. He said that a preacher is hampered and hilt down more than anybody. I 'lowed he wan't—'lowed that you could say putty much what you pleased; said that you could talk about a horse while standin' right up in the pulpit—said that you could mention my horse. He offered to bet five dollars that you wouldn't, and I tuck him up. Now wait a minute. You mention my horse to-night in your sermon, and I'll give you five."

"But I won't encourage betting."

"You won't? But you air encouragin' it when you let fellows go on bettin' without gettin' nipped. You can teach this fellow that it's dangerous to bet, and you might cure him. He thinks he's got a sure thing, and you ought to show him that it's mighty risky even to bet on a certainty, and besides the church will get fixed up."

"You've put it on pretty strong ground, Tobe?"

"Yes, and I believe that's your duty both to the church and to—to showin' fellows that they oughtn't to bet—Well, you know what I'm tryin' to git at."

"Yes, and I will think about it."

That night Tobe leaned forward and listened eagerly to every word the preacher uttered. And he saw no place where a mention of his horse might be slipped in. "The Son of Man came humbly riding on an ass," said the preacher. "How illustrative of his meekness. He could have mounted the charger of a Roman centurion. He could have had the fiery steed from the Arabian desert; or coming down to a mere homelike illustration, he could have ridden an animal such as we see hitched out yonder under the trees, a horse such as our young men ride, such as that poor, blinded sinner Tobe Brock rides. Ah, he is well mounted now on the prancing steed of pride; he feels strong; he thinks that he will never be compelled to flounder on foot in the mud of despair. But his time is coming; and your time is coming, Tom Dabbs; and yours, Lit Perdue; and yours, Sam Johnson; and yours, Bob Stoveall; and yours, John White—yea, you are all approaching your time."

Before the sermon was over every man whom he mentioned was at the bench, praying that his sins might be pardoned; and when the congregation was dismissed, the stake-holder was told to return the money, that the bet was off.

That was a long time ago. Tobe is the pastor of a church in West Tennessee, and Tom is a presiding elder in Arkansas.

Not for Three Hundred Thousand.

AT a watering place in Virginia there arrived one evening a puffy man of middle age, and his daughter, rather an attractive girl. The old man's entrance into society was not upon invitation; it was a break in, as if a steer had jumped into a forbidden pasture. A number of gentlemen and ladies were seated near the end of a shaded veranda, discussing a book that had achieved an almost instant popularity, when the puffy newcomer brusquely shoved his way forward, and in a loud voice blurted out his opinion:

"I ain't read the book," said he, "but I'll bet that it don't amount to much. There is more humbuggery in this here book business than in most any other I know of. Books'll do putty well for women, but in my opinion a man is throwing away his time with 'em. I had a twin brother that took to books along back when he was a boy, and although he was a bright feller—as bright as I was—he never amounted to much. I had to take up a mortgage on his place for him not more'n six months ago. That's about what I think of books." He leaned back against the railing of the "banisters" and surveyed the party with the satisfaction of a man who has carried his point and who is thoroughly prepared for any subsequent attack. The ladies, especially the better-natured ones, smiled; the men, with one exception, laughed. The exception was a young lawyer from Nashville. He looked with the inquiry of disapproval at the intruder, and then quietly remarked:

"I had thought of writing a book, a charming romance, but through fear that I might possibly compel you to take up another mortgage, I will forego the pleasure."

The interloper, no wise abashed, replied: "It's a good step you're takin', I reckon, as the writin' of the book might be more interestin' to you than the readin' of it would be to anybody else."

"Doubtless," retorted the young lawyer, "you are right. Some dull plodder might attempt to spell it out and bruise his alleged mind on unlooked-for, sharp corners."

"Young feller, what is your name?" the intruder asked; and the young fellow, never afraid to make himself known, answered:

"I am George Miles, sir."

"Ah, hah! George Miles. Where do you live?"

"Nashville, sir."

"Ah, hah! I know that town putty well. I went along with the army some little durin' the war, and bought up the hides of the cattle that were killed for the soldiers, and made a pretty good thing out of it in the Nashville market. I used to know an old soap boiler there named Josh Miles. Any kin to him?"

The ladies tittered and the old fellow looked at them in astonishment, knowing that he had not uttered a witticism.

"I never heard of your friend Miles," said the lawyer, "although he might have made a fair article of soap."

"Pity for you then, I reckon, as all men were cleaner for havin' knowed old Josh." The men laughed, the ladies tittered again, and the old fellow, conscious this time that he must have said something to the point, bowed his acknowledgments. Just then his daughter appeared, standing in a door. "Father," she called, "I am ready."

"I am ready, too," he answered, and withdrew with clumsy haste.

That evening, while Miles and several other men sat under a tree, smoking, the old fellow came out with an enormous cigar in his mouth and "squashed" himself down on a bench.

"Boys," said he, breaking into the conversation, "I'm gittin' so I ruther like this here one-hoss place. I did think that it would be a little too much for me to stay out here, and I wa'n't keen to come nuther, but Minnie set her heart on it and away we come. My name is Beck."

No one said anything, and Mr. Beck continued: "I reckon I've done about as much hus'lin' in my time as the most of men. I was a pore boy, but instead of foolin' away my time with books I went to work and ain't sorry for it. I have noticed, in my knockin' round, that money is putty nigh the boss. It may not be happiness in itself, but without it there ain't very much enjoyment. Larnin' may command the respect of the few, but money employs the services of the many, and to challenge the complete respect of men you must make 'em serve you."

"I don't know but you are right," said one of the men.

"Of course I'm right, and what is the use of people shuttin' their eyes against the fact, or ruther pretendin' that they do? I know that there's a sort of respectability, or I mout say aristocracy that money sometimes ain't got, but just wait awhile and money'll git it all right."

"What business are you in?" some one asked.

"Well, I ain't in any business now—have retired, you might say. I made my money in different sorts of speculation and have got it well invested. I live in Georgia and am putty much at home when I'm there, I can tell you. My wife has been dead a good while, and about all I've got to look after is the enjoyment of my daughter. Her will is law with me and I am straightforward enough to say right here, or right anywhere, for that matter, that the man who wins her love will be fortunate. There's about two hundred thousand dollars waitin' for him."

George Miles looked up quickly and, with a sneer, said: "I wouldn't marry her for three hundred thousand."

The old man seized his cane, which he had leaned against the bench and, springing to his feet, glared at Miles, who, without changing his position, sat placidly smoking.

"Do you mean to insult me, sir?" Beck roared.

"Not in the least," Miles answered. "You expressed your opinion and I merely expressed mine. You introduced your daughter's name in a way not only unnecessary to the force of your former statement concerning the power of money, but with a narrow-minded vulgarity that was disgusting. If you want to strike me, do so. I have said nothing in disparagement of the young lady—I said that I wouldn't marry her for three hundred thousand, and I wouldn't; not that she is not worthy of me, but because our tastes are, doubtless, wholly dissimilar. Now, if you want to hit me with that stick, all right."

"I won't hit you," Beck replied. "What you say may be right from your standp'int, but no matter what you thought about my daughter you ought to have kept it to yourself. It looks to me like I would have studied a long time before I would have made any such remark—and I would have thought that any true gentleman would have done the same. I am a rough-and-ready sort of a man, and admit that I don't always do the proper thing, and if my room is worth more to you than my company, why, I wish you good-evenin'."

"Oh, no," several of the men cried, but he brusquely hastened away.

"George, you ought not to have said that," a friend remarked. "You can't blame him for thinking so much of his daughter, nor for his determination to give her future husband two hundred thousand dollars."

"My dear fellow," Miles answered, "I don't blame him for thinking so much of her, and I commend his determination to reward her future husband, but I do despise his vulgar show. He is an old bear, and I want none of him."

"I wouldn't mind marrying the girl," said a young fellow named Hicks; "I could put up with the girl's possible bad taste and with the old man's vulgarity. Yonder go the old man and the girl. He is looking this way, and I warrant he is telling her about you, George."

"I don't care if he is," Miles replied. "His ill-will and her prejudice can't hurt me."

CHAPTER II.

SEVERAL days later Miles, whose friends had left the place, was strolling along the mountain's side when suddenly, upon turning a sharp point of rock that jutted out over the path, he met Miss Beck. The path was too narrow to admit of his passing the girl, and he was about to turn back, when she pleasantly remarked:

"Oh, don't turn back on my account. I will swing over to one side and let you pass. I shouldn't have far to fall, you see."

"I'll hang over," said he, bowing.

"Oh, no," she interposed. "I am afraid you might hurt yourself, and then——"

"And then what?" he asked.

"Nothing, only you might be disfigured if you should chance to fall, and you might afterward consent to marry a girl for less than three hundred thousand dallars."

"Ah, your father repeated my remark," he said, slightly coloring.

"Yes, or I shouldn't have known of it, as I wasn't eavesdropping."

He would gladly have tumbled off to let her pass, but she detained him with this remark:

"You place a pretty high estimate upon yourself, don't you?"

"Yes, rather," he answered, now determined to be bold.

"It is strange that I never heard of you," she said. "I was looking over a sort of encyclopedia of great men just before I came here, and it is singular that your picture was not in it."

"The compiler of the book called on me," he replied, "but I refused to become the victim of a cheap print. He wanted my picture, and had intended that it should fill one page and run over on the second, but I refused."

"And I suppose," said the girl, "that if he had thought of putting in your self-importance, he would have counted on filling the entire book."

"I don't know, but if he had done so, his volume would have been more respectable."

"Oh, it must be delightful to be so respectable," she exclaimed, with enthusiasm. "By the way, who was your father?"

"His name is Andrew Miles."

"What does he do?"

"He is a lawyer."

"Ah! A strange country this, where the aristocracy is composed mainly of lawyers. What was your grandfather, or did you ever hear of him?"

Miles blushed. He had heard more or less vaguely, of one of his grandfathers—had heard that he was a cobbler and that he had deserted from the army during the war of 1812.

"Oh, don't tax your memory with trying to recall his name. I am so glad to have met you," she suddenly exclaimed. "I like to see gentleness and consideration joined with greatness. Now, sir, if you feel disposed to scramble down you would oblige me by doing so."

* * * * * *

The season was growing late, and there were but few visitors remaining. Miles continued to linger, partly because it made but little difference where he was, and partly because he didn't want that Miss Beck to think that she had driven him off. He met her every day, and spoke, in reply to her, his little piece of sarcasm. One day while the girl was playing on the piano he strode into the parlor. She ceased playing upon seeing him, and turning, said:

"I don't object to mild punishment, but I will not torture you with my music."

" You are becoming considerate as the days pass by."

" Yes, and I am tired of playing, anyway. Isn't it a great pity that father isn't worth four hundred thousand dollars."

" Why so?"

" Because he might then be able to marry me off."

" Possibly. Some men are not very particular."

" And," said she, " I am convinced that the majority of women are not particular at all."

The old man appeared in the door. His face was haggard and a wild look was in his eyes.

" Minnie," he called, " Minnie, come here."

She ran to him and Miles heard him say, "I am ruined. That iron company is busted up and I am ruined."

* * * * * *

It was rather late at night. The Becks were arranging their departure. Miles was sitting in the parlor when Miss Beck entered. Seeing him, she drew back and was about to withdraw, when he bade her stay a moment.

" You must excuse me," she said. " I do not care to hear any sarcasm to-night; I don't believe I could stand it. I am very wretched on my father's account. He has been victimized and is now a pauper."

" And are you not wretched on your own account?" he asked.

"Please don't gibe me now," she pleaded.

He got up and moving slowly toward her, said: "I am no better than one of my grandfathers, and he was shot for desertion. I have been a prig, a brute, and now I will give you the opportunity to humiliate me. I love you."

She said nothing—she stood as if stunned, but her eyes spoke and he put his arms about her.

"It—it will make that poor old man happy again," she said. "It will make him happy for he knows that I love you."

HER SWEET DREAM.

MANY a season had passed since any one had ventured to teach a school in the Black-Haw neighborhood. The old log house wherein so many droning voices had in times gone by parsed "John found his hat in the road," had begun to squat with the weight of time resting upon it; hazel-bushes grew about the doorstep, and a grape-vine, crawling on the ground, passed a dozen sassafras saplings to droop over the window. It is said that Henry Clay once "taught a term" in this house, but of this there is no direct proof, though it is well authenticated that Tom Marshall came hither at night to join in debate with the wiseacres of the community. After the war the Black-Haw community lost its ambition; the old men were cowed, and the young men went West, and during ten years the schoolhouse was idle. Then came along a spry young man who said that he wanted to earn money enough to finish his own education. He mounted a horse and circulated a paper. Some families subscribed a scholar, some a half, and some but a third; but he gathered what might have been regarded as a fair sprinkling, and opened up his school. Perhaps his own education was finished, though of this nothing is known, but it is known that he did not earn the money in that neighborhood; for on the third morning after he took his place beside the great flagstone hearth, a lout of a youngster clothed in brown jeans came up and declared that it was all right to study and make pot-hooks with pokeberry ink, but that the time to treat had come.

"Treat!" exclaimed the teacher, and his eyes stuck out. "I haven't enough money to buy a handkerchief; so don't come to me with a proposition to treat."

The boy said that he was sorry that the teacher had no handkerchief; he reckoned that every educated man ought to have one, but at the same time if education couldn't furnish a man with a handkerchief, what was the use of spending half a lifetime in getting an education?

The teacher ordered him to sit down. He was rather a polite boy, and he did not positively refuse, but he demurred. He said that he wasn't at all tired; said that he had been sitting down all day. No, he didn't want to sit down; he wanted to eat.

The crossroads grocer, not more than five miles away, had cove oysters and cheese, and a council of four had decided that the teacher must trudge over to the store, accompanied by an escort of honor, and purchase specified material for a small feast. The council knew that times were hard, and therefore would not insist that the entire school be invited to the feast; indeed, the council insisted upon a feast for the council.

The teacher's smile was yellowish and sickly; he said that he appreciated the generosity of the council, but that modesty compelled him to decline the escort of honor.

A few more remarks were made, and then an ancient dust began to arise from the floor. Along toward noon the young man stepped out of the schoolroom, with the back of his coat sliced like a gridiron; after that, year after year, the old house was empty.

One afternoon, not long ago, a young woman called at the house of Clab Morris, and said that she had come to teach school in the old house. The visitor had just sat down upon a bench which Clab had drawn out from the wall, and she did not see him when he turned his face away to laugh; but she must have heard his snicker, for she looked at him sharply when he gave her his attention again. She was young, rather frail and pretty. She was dressed in bright colors, and looked like a part of the springtime, just come, and just beginning to green the hillsides.

"Well," said Clab, "I've got no objections."

"I thank you. I was told that you were about the most influential man in the neighborhood——"

"Yes," he broke in; "I reckon I am. Don't know Lit Smith, I guess?"

"No, sir."

"Well, I can fling him down three times outen five, any day, and a man that can do that has got influence, I tell you. Still, I ain't proud, and you neenter hesitate to talk to me jest as you feel."

She smiled, and replied: "It is rare that one meets with such modesty."

"Yes, I reckon it is. Folks these days brag a monst'us sight; but I allus made it a p'int to be modest. You'll sorter have to excuse things around here; wife has gone over to one of the neighbor's, and won't be back for an hour or so; children all growed up and gone. Now, what is your idee of teachin' of a school?"

She explained that she would teach good manners, as well as reading and writing, and he nodded his head in approval.

"Good manners," he said, "is a mighty fine thing. Goin' along the road the other day, and one of Phil Mayhew's boys flung a rock at me, and pecked a hole in my old mar's head. And I should think that sich a youngster was somewhat lackin' in good manners, wouldn't you?"

She agreed that she thought so, and the affinity thus established greatly pleased him. He said he would do all he could to assist her in getting up the school.

"But I don't see why you want to teach school," he added. "I allus thought women that couldn't git married was the ones that teached school; but it strikes me that you could marry about any man that might happen to come along. Them eyes of your'n look like violets a-peepin' outen the snow. Thar, now, 'skuze me; didn't mean no harm. But I mean it when I say you could marry most anybody. Why, my son Zeb, the hoss doctor, would break his neck atter you, 'cause he's a good jedge of fine stock, and I want to tell you that a hoss has to be monst'us sick to git away from him. Yes, you'd ketch any man's eye, and ef I wa'n't married—but I don't want to brag. Now tell me a leetle somethin' about yourself."

"Must I be perfectly frank with you?"

"I don't know what you mean, but I think you ought to."

"I will. I live quite a distance from here. A young man and I had a quarrel, and I have come away to teach school."

"Ah, ha! and I don't reckon the young man was yo' brother. That's all right. I've got a good deal of sympathy for folks that have quarrels. Don't say nothin' about it, but some time ago wife an' me had a quarrel, and I'm big enough to say that it was mostly my fault. I tuck a lot of her carpet-rags to wash off a hoss with, and she felt insulted, and I did, too, when she did, and so we had it. Well, I didn't go off to teach school, but I went out into the woods and swore that I'd sleep thar behind a log till she 'pologized, and she 'lowed that ef I waited for that I'd lay thar as long as the log did, and so we had it. I raked up some leaves and lay down behind the log, and that evenin' she brought my supper, and I lay thar and eat it, and wiped my hands on the leaves, and 'lowed that everything was all right. I slept first-rate, and the next mornin' I went about my business as usual, and the next night I tuck my place behind the log. About nine o'clock she come out and asked me ef I had kiver enough, and I told her that I believed not; so she raked up a few more leaves and put 'em on me, and went on back to the house. Well, I got along all right till about twelve o'clock, and then come the coldest rain you ever seed; and jest about the time I got soakin' wet it turned off into a freeze, and then I 'lowed that it was about time for me to 'pologize, and I got outen that pile of leaves and walked home like a board, and since then I've let her carpet-rags alone, I tell you. Why, bless my life, and your'n, too, yander she comes now."

Again on the playground there were shouts of laughter and the soft patter of bare feet, and a favorite with everyone was Miss Elmer, the teacher. The larger boys were at work in the fields, hastening to plant the crops, and there among the hazel-bushes and the vines the young woman worked and dreamed. Nearly every day, at playtime, sitting where the light was mellow, she would write a letter, but she always tore it to pieces when "books" were called.

"What makes you write so much and tear it up?" a little girl asked. "Why don't you come and play with us?"

And the teacher answered, "I am writing a dream that came to me and went away again."

"And do you keep on writing it, hoping it will come back?" an older girl asked.

But the young woman shook her head, and told them that they must talk no more about it. But the next day she would write another letter. Once she put her writing into an envelope, and gave it to old Clab to post; but she ran after him, took it, and tore it into pieces, red with blushes, as she scattered the fragments in the road.

Clab's wife knew that a man was at the bottom of the young woman's trouble.

"My dear," she said one morning, just as Miss Elmer was getting ready for school, "I wouldn't pester myself with writin' so much; it's about a fetch-taked man, and I know it; and I want to tell you that there is hardly one of them that's worth the powder and lead to kill 'em. They do provoke a body so, a-sp'ilin' carpet-rags and a-wallerin' behind logs in the pouts; so ef I was you I would jest go ahead with my school, and let him alone, whoever he may be. Here comes Sam Briley."

Briley was the mental mystery of the neighborhood; he was called inoffensive, but Miss Elmer was afraid of him. Often at night he would come to the house, and sitting with his eyes fastened on her, would say the oddest things.

"I'll walk down to the schoolhouse with you," he said, nodding at old Clab's wife, and then shooting a gaze at the teacher.

She was afraid to refuse, so she walked on, saying nothing. He walked beside her.

"Did you write you' long letter yistidy?" he asked.

" Yes, sir."

" What for?"

" To tear up."

" What you want to write it fur, if you tear it up?"

" Because I feel like writing it, and then I feel like tearing it up."

" I don't like it."

" *You* don't like it!"

"That's what I said."

"What have you to do with it?"

"A good deal; don't want you to write to a man."

She looked at him, walking along; she moved further away from him, but he stepped up close beside her.

"I ain't told you yet," he said, "but I had a dream, too. Heard you say that you had one. And in my dream I heard a voice say that you was made for me, and not for the man that you write letters to."

"Mr. Briley, will you please go away?"

"Yes, I'll do that; but you musn't expect me to stay away. They say that I went crazy on religion, and I 'lowed that they might be right, but now I know they was wrong. I went crazy about you, years before I saw you, and my dream tells me that you can bring my mind back and make me happy. Will you?"

She looked at him. They were standing still, facing each other. His face was pale, and his eyes looked like coals of fire in a bed of ashes. She was frightened.

"Don't try to run away from me," he said; "I can run faster than you can, but I won't pass you; I'll keep up with you, and we'll run on to the end of the rainbow together. I'll let you go now, but to-night I'll come to the house and tell you more about my plans."

He turned away, and she hastened to the school. At

playtime she sat alone, dreaming her dream, but it was fitful with the image of the crazy man flitting through it. A little girl came up to her, hanging back, and stammering.

"What is the trouble, Mollie?" she asked.

"If I tell you you'll whip me," the child replied.

"No, I won't."

"It was awful bad, but I did it."

"Did what?"

"Sent the pieces of letter. You took the letter from old Caleb and tore it to pieces and threw the pieces in the road; but you didn't tear the envelope very much, and I took all the pieces and found the name on the envelope, and put all the pieces in another envelope, and wrote the name on it, and put it in the post office because it made me sorry to see you writing all the time. And now are you going to whip me?"

The teacher could scarcely speak. "Run on away," she sobbed.

The children were dismissed and in a corner where the light was soft the teacher sat dreaming. But in the dream was the image of the insane man, and she felt that he was at the house, waiting for her. She dreaded to meet him again. An hour passed but she did not write—she sat there dreaming. During the day there had been a hoarse wind in the tree tops; now it was a whisper among the bushes. Suddenly she was startled by a footstep at the door. She sprung to her feet to run away, but a voice commanded her to stay. The insane man stood at the threshold; in his hand he held an enormous bludgeon.

"Stand right where you are," he commanded, advancing into the room.

She stood there, trembling. He halted in front of the long writing table and placed his club upon it.

"Don't move," he said. For a time he was silent and then he continued: "I have had another dream and this time it was perfectly clear. At first I thought that to save my life you had to be my wife, but my dream tells me better."

"Oh, thank you," she cried.

"But hold on. You are not to save me that way, but you are to save me after all. The blood of the lamb taketh away the sin of the world. You are the lamb and I am the world. And your blood must wash away my sins. You are saved already for you are a lamb, but I am condemned for I am the world and therefore full of sin. But even a lamb must pray, and now———" With his finger nail he made a mark in the soft wood of the table. "And now, when the sun gets here, you must die."

She was a brave little creature. She did not scream; she would argue with him. The sun was going fast and the light had but an inch to move. She looked at the light—looked at the club which he had taken up.

"When it reaches this mark there will be two blows," he said, "one on the table as the signal and the other on——"

"I understand," she interrupted, "but you must know that it is not necessary for me to die in order to save you. I can save you better by living."

"No," he replied, shaking his head, "my dream tells me not."

"But I have had a dream, and it tells me that I must live for you, not die for you."

"Your dream is a lie; mine is the truth."

"But," she persisted, "my dream says that yours is a lie. Let us go to the house and compare them."

He shook his head. "No, dreams are nothing when you begin to compare them."

"Why, they told me that you were a half-wit and here you are talking wisdom," she cried.

He nodded his head and looked down at the mark.

"They told you the truth," he said. "But sometimes a half-wit is better than a whole wit. Let me see." He unbuttoned his coat. "I must dye the bosom of my shirt with your blood—and it will be beautiful. Don't you wish you could see it? Oh, you are a beautiful creature. And ain't it right that you should pay the penalty for such beauty? How things do change. This morning I wanted you for my wife, but now I want your beautiful blood. Yesterday I was a fool, spluttering a fool's words, but now I am a wise man with a strange fire in my breast. And I believe that when I go out of here with my bosom dyed with your precious blood——" He hesitated, gazing down upon the table, but the light was gone; a fleck of cloud had dimmed the sun. "It will be back in a moment," he said.

The light came back. It was almost touching the mark. "Let me pray," she said, sinking upon her knees as she saw him grasp the club. After all it was not so hard to die. She had nothing to live for. The madman struck the desk. The next blow—it did not fall. She waited, praying, afraid to look up. The terrific blow upon the table had deafened her, and she heard nothing more, no footsteps, no struggle, no fall upon the floor—nothing. Something touched her hair. She sprung to her feet and a young man seized her in his arms.

At the door they halted and looked back. The madman lay sprawled upon the floor with his arms spread out. They did not speak, both silently wondering if he were dead. The madman groaned, and the young man and the teacher, with a look of relief, hastened away.

" Your torn letter——"

"The mischief of a blessed child," she broke in. "But let us say nothing now."

They passed a log house and a little girl ran out. The teacher, with tears in her eyes, took the little thing in her arms and kissed her passionately. "Oh, you have brought back my sweet dream," she said.

THE END.

www.ingramcontent.com/pod-product-compliance
Lightning Source LLC
Chambersburg PA
CBHW020904230426
43666CB00008B/1302